Contents

Introduction: to the teacher

Poetry offers a range of possible responses for the student, and consequently much scope for the teacher. Here is a brief summary of some such responses:

—discussion of a poem in pairs, groups or as a class
—reporting back to the class on a discussion
—reading aloud on tape, as a class, or for performance
—further reading
—informal written responses, like logs, journal entries, records of first impressions, notes
—formal written responses, like essays or imaginative writing based in some way upon a text or theme
—anthology making

If this anthology is being used with fifth year classes, we assume that there will be increased focus on formal work in preparation for GCSE examinations at 16+, whether in the form of folder work or as a build-up to tackling the 'unseen' poem on examination papers; but we urge teachers to remember that poetry can also provide excellent material for oral work in the later as well as the early stages of such a course. To these ends we have included a new section on 'Approaching the Unseen Poem' and reprinted from Volume 1 the section of 'Ideas for Coursework Folders'.

The notes that follow the poems in each section of the anthology also reflect the needs of this latter half of the course. There is more attention devoted to the language of the poems themselves than in Volume 1, just as many questions in examination papers move toward that kind of appreciation at this stage. It follows that our notes have a differentiated structure: whereas in Volume 1 the notes focussed on problems of literal and deductive comprehension and then provided suggestions for further responses, in Volume 2 we have added to these suggestions some questions that aim to elicit an evaluative response.

It is for this reason that we end the anthology with 'Poems for Comparison'. Here students can exercise their ability to read at the literal and deductive levels, and by comparing the way different writers handle the same subject or theme, can extend their understanding to the evaluative level. This is a logical conclusion to a course that began at the beginning of Volume 1 with poetry that used the raw material of the senses.

POETRY
HORIZONS

Volume 2

Edited by
Richard Andrews
and
Ian Bentley

Bell & Hyman

Published in 1988 by
Bell & Hyman
An imprint of Unwin Hyman
Denmark House
37–39 Queen Elizabeth Street
London SE1 2QB

British Library Cataloguing in Publication Data
Poetry horizons.
    1. English poetry
    I. Andrews, Richard   II. Bentley, Ian
    821′.008′09282   PR1175

    ISBN 0–7135–2679–3 v.1
    ISBN 0–7135–2680–7 v.2

Designed by Geoffrey Wadsley
Typeset by Latimer Trend & Company Ltd,
Plymouth
Printed in Great Britain by
R. J. Acford Ltd, Chichester

List of Poems

* Key poem

Section 3: Political

Section 4: Featured Poets

List of Illustrations

Self Portrait, 1973, by Francis Bacon, Private Collection, London; p6

Double Marlon, 1966, by Andy Warhol © DACS; p26

Communist and Socialist (Second Version), 1979, by R. B. Kitaj, Marlborough Fine Art (London) Ltd; p52

John Betjeman, detail of photograph for Picture Post by Kurt Hutton, © BBC Hulton Picture Library; *Sylvia Plath*, detail of photograph by Rollie McKenna, courtesy of Faber & Faber Ltd, by permission of Olwyn Hughes; *Langston Hughes*, detail of photograph courtesy of the New York Public Library, Schomburg Center for Research in Black Culture; p86

SCHWITTERS, 1959, Evident poem, and *MARINETTI, 1959, Evident poem*, by Jiří Kolář, photographs courtesy of the Albemarle Gallery, London; p116

Section 1

Reflecting

Self Portrait
Francis Bacon

I can never sit down and decide to write a poem. If I have a book review to do then I can do that any time. I do not particularly like the word inspiration but, nevertheless, the writing of a poem is for me, and I am sure for other poets, something that I have to wait for. Coleridge, who wrote 'Kubla Khan' and 'The Ancient Mariner', said of the act of making a poem that it is accompanied by 'a more than usual excitement and a more than usual sense of order'. That is the best definition I know.

There are several ways in which I write and they are all in some way linked. Sometimes I have an odd feeling of excitement in my stomach very like the feeling of 'butterflies' we have when we are nervous; at other times the opening line of a poem seems to leap into mind. Whatever the sign of a poem on the way may be, I always have to have a pencil or biro and a piece of paper. I cannot keep a poem in my head. Geoffrey Hill once told me that a whole poem would *sing* inside his head. I can write almost anywhere but not when there is the sound of pop music bellowing around me.

I write most of my poems at night, perhaps because there is a tangible sense of peace then and also because my mind and imagination come to life in the evening and late at night. I do not write many drafts of one poem but go through several, sometimes many, whole poems before I know by instinct that the right one has come; it is then written out almost without alteration. I can only re-member how a poem came if there is something unusual about the place or time in which I wrote it.

For example, I had been thinking for a long time about power, physical power, political power, power that one person has over another. The right poem suddenly came when I was in Rome and it was called 'Fountain'. I had found the perfect image here because I had seen so many in Rome. I quickly wrote the poem down on Maundy Thursday before I went to the Holy Week ceremonies at one of the great basilicas. I felt very happy and also very grateful.

One thing I do remember about 'Absence' is the person who prompted the poem. I was on the edge of being in love with him, but it never came to anything.

One hint of a poem's authenticity is for me when it easily gives itself a title. In a way, there is more pain about writing poems than delight; so often I feel I shall never write again. When a poem does arrive I write it out at great speed, and afterwards have a wonderful feeling of release.

Whence the springs of poems arise I do not know. They may come from our unconsciousness and yet I feel that there is something of divinity about poetry. One is lucky if one has the gift but the flow can be stopped by alcohol, worldliness, sometimes even by public success. Poetry always demands vigilance and dedication. The craft of it must be cared for, kept in good working order for when the next poem comes.

ELIZABETH JENNINGS

7

A Study Of Reading Habits

When getting my nose in a book
Cured most things short of school,
It was worth ruining my eyes
To know I could still keep cool,
And deal out the old right hook
To dirty dogs twice my size.

Later, with inch-thick specs,
Evil was just my lark:
Me and my cloak and fangs
Had ripping times in the dark.   10
The women I clubbed with sex!
I broke them up like meringues.

Don't read much now: the dude
Who lets the girl down before
The hero arrives, the chap
Who's yellow and keeps the store,
Seem far too familiar. Get stewed:
Books are a load of crap.

Philip Larkin

Monotony

One monotonous day follows another
identically monotonous. The same things
will happen to us again and again,
the same moments come and go.

A month passes by, brings another month.
Easy to guess what lies ahead:
all of yesterday's boredom.
And tomorrow ends up no longer like tomorrow.

C. P. Cavafy

Tombstone Library

In Tombstone there was, it seems,
a public library
between the marshall's office
and the Silver Lode Saloon
On endless, silent afternoons
the clicking of the faro wheel
the tired piano's nervous tinkle
scratching the library's wooden walls
I like to think of them
the whores and gamblers   *10*
the faro dealers and the mining men
cool in the library's silent shade
whispering their way through 'Romance'
and 'Ancient History'
soft spurs jingling past the rows of books
the half-breed coughing gently over 'War and Peace'
And at the issue desk
a stocky figure in a bowler hat
'I'm sorry Mr Earp, this book is overdue'
He bends and fumbles   *20*
flicks out a coin, smiles
(his teeth are not yet film-star white)
dark and nervous as a cat
He turns and moves towards 'Mythology'

Richard Hill

The Mosquito Knows

The mosquito knows full well, small as he is
he's a beast of prey.
But after all
he only takes his bellyful,
he doesn't put my blood in the bank.

D. H. Lawrence

9

Paltry-Looking People

And think how the nightingale, who is so shy,
makes of himself a belfry of throbbing sound!
While people mince mean words through their teeth.

And think how wild animals trot with splendour
till man destroys them!
how vividly they make their assertion of life!

But how paltry, mingy and dingy and squalid people look
in their rag garments scuttling through the streets,
or sitting stuck like automata in automobiles!

D. H. Lawrence

Absence

I visited the place where we last met.
Nothing was changed, the gardens were well-tended,
The fountains sprayed their usual steady jet;
There was no sign that anything had ended
And nothing to instruct me to forget.

The thoughtless birds that shook out of the trees,
Singing an ecstasy I could not share,
Played cunning in my thoughts. Surely in these
Pleasures there could not be a pain to bear
Or any discord shake the level breeze.   *10*

It was because the place was just the same
That made your absence seem a savage force,
For under all the gentleness there came
An earthquake tremor: fountain, birds and grass
Were shaken by my thinking of your name.

Elizabeth Jennings

It Rains

It rains, and nothing stirs within the fence
Anywhere through the orchard's untrodden, dense
Forest of parsley. The great diamonds
Of rain on the grassblades there is none to break,
Or the fallen petals further down to shake.

And I am nearly as happy as possible
To search the wilderness in vain though well,
To think of two walking, kissing there,
Drenched, yet forgetting the kisses of the rain:
Sad, too, to think that never, never again,   *10*

Unless alone, so happy shall I walk
In the rain. When I turn away, on its fine stalk
Twilight has fined to naught, the parsley flower
Figures, suspended still and ghostly white,
The past hovering as it revisits the light.

Edward Thomas

The Street

A long and silent street.
I walk in blackness and I stumble and fall
and rise, and I walk blind, my feet
stepping on silent stones and dry leaves.
Someone behind me also stepping on stones, leaves:
if I slow down, he slows;
if I run, he runs. I turn: nobody.
Everything dark and doorless.
Turning and turning among these corners
which lead forever to the street   *10*
where nobody waits for, nobody follows me,
where I pursue a man who stumbles
and rises and says when he sees me: nobody.

Octavio Paz

Because

My father and my mother never quarrelled.
They were united in a kind of love
As daily as the *Sydney Morning Herald*,
Rather than like the eagle or the dove.

I never saw them casually touch,
Or show a moment's joy in one another.
Why should this matter to me now so much?
I think it bore more hardly on my mother,

Who had more generous feelings to express.
My father had dammed up his Irish blood 10
Against all drinking praying fecklessness,
And stiffened into stone and creaking wood.

His lips would make a switching sound, as though
Spontaneous impulse must be kept at bay.
That it was mainly weakness I see now,
But then my feelings curled back in dismay.

Small things can pit the memory like a cyst:
Having seen other fathers greet their sons,
I put my childish face up to be kissed
After an absence. The rebuff still stuns 20

My blood. The poor man's curt embarrassment
At such a delicate proffer of affection
Cut like a saw. But home the lesson went:
My tenderness thenceforth escaped detection.

My mother sang *Because*, and *Annie Laurie*,
White Wings, and other songs; her voice was sweet.
I never gave enough, and I am sorry;
But we were all closed in the same defeat.

People do what they can; they were good people,
They cared for us and loved us. Once they stood 30
Tall in my childhood as the school, the steeple.
How can I judge without ingratitude?

Judgment is simply trying to reject
A part of what we are because it hurts.
The living cannot call the dead collect:
They won't accept the charge, and it reverts.

It's my own judgment day that I draw near,
Descending in the past, without a clue,
Down to that central deadness: the despair
Older than any hope I ever knew.   *40*

James McAuley

Brooklyn Cop

Built like a gorilla but less timid,
thick-fleshed, steak-coloured, with two
hieroglyphs in his face that mean
trouble, he walks the sidewalk and the
thin tissue over violence. This morning
when he said, 'See you, babe' to his wife,
he hoped it, he truly hoped it.
He is a gorilla
to whom 'Hiya, honey' is no cliché.

Should the tissue tear, should he plunge through   *10*
into violence, what clubbings, what
gunshots between Phoebe's
Whamburger and Louie's Place.

Who would be him, gorilla with a nightstick,
whose home is a place
he might, this time, never get back to?

And who would be who have to be
his victims?

Norman MacCaig

13

Bags Of Meat

'Here's a fine bag of meat,'
Says the master-auctioneer,
As the timid, quivering steer,
Starting a couple of feet
At the prod of a drover's stick,
And trotting lightly and quick,
A ticket stuck on his rump,
Enters with a bewildered jump.

'Where he's lived lately, friends,
I'd live till lifetime ends: 10
They've a whole life everyday
Down there in the Vale, have they!
He'd be worth the money to kill
And give away Christmas for goodwill.

'Now here's a heifer—worth more
Than bid, were she bone-poor;
Yet she's round as a barrel of beer';
'She's a plum,' said the second auctioneer.

'Now this young bull—for thirty pound?
Worth that to manure your ground!'   20
'Or to stand,' chimed the second one,
'And have his picter done!'

The beast was rapped on the horns and snout
To make him turn about.
'Well,' cried a buyer, 'another crown—
Since I've dragged here from Taunton Town!'

'That calf, she sucked three cows,
Which is not matched for bouse
In the nurseries of high life
By the first-born of a nobleman's wife!'   30
The stick falls, meaning, 'A true tale's told,'
On the buttock of the creature sold,
And the buyer leans over and snips
His mark on one of the animal's hips.

Each beast, when driven in,
Looks round at the ring of bidders there
With a much-amazed reproachful stare,
    As at unnatural kin,
For bringing him to a sinister scene
So strange, unhomelike, hungry, mean;   *40*
His fate the while suspended between
    A butcher, to kill out of hand,
    And a farmer, to keep on the land;
One can fancy a tear runs down his face
When the butcher wins, and he's driven from the place.

Thomas Hardy

One Flesh

Lying apart now, each in a separate bed,
He with a book, keeping the light on late,
She like a girl dreaming of childhood,
All men elsewhere—it is as if they wait
Some new event: the book he holds unread,
Her eyes fixed on the shadows overhead.

Tossed up like flotsam from a former passion,
How cool they lie. They hardly ever touch,
Or if they do it is like a confession
Of having little feeling—or too much.   *10*
Chastity faces them, a destination
For which their whole lives were a preparation.

Strangely apart and strangely close together,
Silence between them like a thread to hold
And not wind in. And time itself's a feather
Touching them gently. Do they know they're old,
These two who are my father and my mother
Whose fire, from which I came, has now grown cold?

Elizabeth Jennings

15

Work And Play

The swallow of summer, she toils all summer,
A blue-dark knot of glittering voltage,
A whiplash swimmer, a fish of the air.
    But the serpent of cars that crawls through the dust
    In shimmering exhaust
    Searching to slake
    Its fever in ocean
    Will play and be idle or else it will bust.

The swallow of summer, the barbed harpoon,
She flings from the furnace, a rainbow of purples,   10
Dips her glow in the pond and is perfect.
    But the serpent of cars that collapsed at the beach
    Disgorges its organs
    A scamper of colours
    Which roll like tomatoes
    Nude as tomatoes
    With sand in their creases
    To cringe in the sparkle of rollers and screech.

The swallow of summer, the seamstress of summer,
She scissors the blue into shapes and she sews it,   20
She draws a long thread and she knots it at corners.
    But the holiday people
    Are laid out like wounded
    Flat as in ovens
    Roasting and basting
    With faces of torment as space burns them blue
    Their heads are transistors
    Their teeth grit on sand grains
    Their lost kids are squalling
    While man-eating flies   30
    Jab electric shock needles but what can they do?

They can climb in their cars with raw bodies, raw faces
    And start up the serpent
    And headache it homeward
    A car full of squabbles
    And sobbing and stickiness
    With sand in their crannies

Inhaling petroleum
That pours from the foxgloves
While the evening swallow   40
The swallow of summer, cartwheeling through crimson,
Touches the honey-slow river and turning
Returns to the hand stretched from under the eaves—
A boomerang of rejoicing shadow.

Ted Hughes

The Potato Patch

In those days there was a god,
and the thought rinsed her mind leaving

it clear: had the island disappeared
with its god? Certainly, she'd never

see either again. Would her potato-
patch be recognizable after 20 years—

what shape would it be, eroded,
at the bottom of the sea? Maureen looks

at the window-box of her new flat
and knows someone has played a practical   10

joke: will there be a hoe in the broom-
cupboard, a pig or bearded goat tied

to the bus-stop outside, waiting
to be fed? The last tenants were city-

bred children obeying their private
call to nature: would their potatoes

turn up at the local greengrocer's
and remind her that she was far from home?

E. A. Markham

Night Rain

What time of night it is
I do not know
Except that like some fish
Doped out of the deep
I have bobbed up bellywise
From stream of sleep
And no cocks crow.
It is drumming hard here
And I suppose everywhere
Droning with insistent ardour upon   *10*
Our roof-thatch and shed
And through sheaves slit open
To lightning and rafters
I cannot make out overhead
Great water drops are dribbling
Falling like orange or mango
Fruits showered forth in the wind
Or perhaps I should say so
Much like beads I could in prayer tell
Them on string as they break   *20*
In wooden bowls and earthenware
Mother is busy now deploying
About our roomlet and floor.
Although it is so dark
I know her practised step as
She moves her bins, bags, and vats
Out of the run of water
That like ants filing out of the wood
Will scatter and gain possession
Of the floor. Do not tremble then   *30*
But turn brothers, turn upon your side
Of the loosening mats
To where the others lie.
We have drunk tonight of a spell
Deeper than the owl's or bat's
That wet of wings may not fly.
Bedraggled upon the *iroko*, they stand
Emptied of hearts, and
Therefore will not stir, no, not
Even at dawn for then   *40*

They must scurry in to hide.
So we'll roll over on our back
And again roll to the beat
Of drumming all over the land
And under its ample soothing hand
Joined to that of the sea
We will settle to sleep of the innocent and free.

John Pepper Clark

Holidays In Childhood

Last year Harold was making a boat
For his small cousin from the north country.
His tools and timber were not very good,
But he had clever fingers, the youth Harold,
And he had shaped the hull with all his skill,
Given it narrow lines to slip through water,
And cut the keel to give a seabird's poise.
The hull was finished, mast and bowsprit fitted,
Waiting for halyards, blocks, sails fore and aft
To change the shaven wood into a yacht.   10
It was going to be a trim and speedy ship.

The hull is in the outhouse now,
With the thick knife beside it.
It still looks like a swift and sturdy vessel,
And its prow seems eager for the waves.
The mountain still looms distantly beyond the town,
With the sky above it, and the strong winds
Whistling in the grasses as they always whistle.
The shops and houses are all just the same,
And the trams rattle by as they did last year—   20
Though this year Harold is dead.

Clifford Dyment

Opposition

In my youth
I was opposed to school.
And now, again,
I'm opposed to work.

Above all it is health
And righteousness that I hate the most.
There's nothing so cruel to man
as health and honesty.

Of course I'm opposed to 'the Japanese spirit'
And duty and human feeling make me vomit.   *10*
I'm against any government anywhere
And show my bum to authors' and artists' circles.

When I'm asked for what I was born,
Without scruple, I'll reply, 'To oppose.'
When I'm in the east
I want to go to the west.

I fasten my coat at the left, my shoes right and left.
My *hakama* I wear back to front and I ride a horse
     facing its buttocks.
What everyone else hates I like
And my greatest hate of all is people feeling the same.   *20*

This I believe: to oppose
Is the only fine thing in life.
To oppose is to live.
To oppose is to get a grip on the very self.

Kaneko Mitsuharu

Notes and activities

How to Use the notes and activities
*Term included in the Glossary

The *Questions to discuss* are for oral work either in class or in smaller groups.

The sections of notes in italics suggest possible writing activities arising from each poem.

The key poems between double rules have more detailed notes and might form the focus of your coursework.

A Study Of Reading Habits   *Philip Larkin*
'Get stewed': 1960s slang for 'Get drunk', but it also meant 'Get lost'

Questions to discuss
What age would you say the speaker in the poem is? And how far back is he looking?
If the poem is about reading, why does the speaker end with 'Books are a load of crap'?
What do you notice about the title?
What would you say the tone of this poem is?

You will no doubt notice a difference in the language between this poem and, say, 'It Rains'. Look up the following words in a dictionary and then divide them into two columns, one applying to the Thomas poem, and one to Larkin's:

formal, colloquial, casual, poetic, slangy, informal, romantic, down-to-earth

Can you find examples of each? (See **Tone** *in the Glossary at the end of this book.)*

Monotony   *C. P. Cavafy*
Cavafy was a Greek writer who wrote mostly in Alexandria on the north coast of Egypt.

Questions to discuss
A straightforward poem, but can you explain the apparent contradiction in the last line, '. . . tomorrow ends up no longer like tomorrow'?

You might like to try a piece of writing — poetry or prose — with the title 'Tomorrow'. To get you started, write the word in the middle of a large piece of paper and note down as many associations as spring to mind. Then piece them together and build up your work.

Tombstone Library   *Richard Hill*
'faro': a game of chance played by betting on the order of appearance of certain cards

Questions to discuss
Tombstone is a town in the Wild West, but why do you think the poet has chosen this particular town as the location and title of his poem?
Why does Earp "move towards 'Mythology'" at the end of the poem?

What effect is the writer trying to create by having a hero like Wyatt Earp return an overdue book to the local library?

The Mosquito Knows   *D. H. Lawrence*
Paltry-Looking People   *D. H. Lawrence*
These are both from Lawrence's collection *Pansies* (from the French 'pensées' = thoughts)
'my blood in the bank': not a blood-bank, of course!

Questions to discuss
What is Lawrence suggesting about people and creatures in these poems?
What are the particular targets in each poem?

Why do you think Lawrence did not use rhyme here? What effect does he create by not using rhyme?

It Rains   *Edward Thomas*
'fined to nought': refined to nothing. The twilight makes it appear that the cow parsley flower is hovering in mid-air, because you cannot see its stalk in the dim light.

Questions to discuss
What is the poet remembering?
The words 'sad' and 'happy' figure in this poem, but is it a 'sad' or 'happy' poem? How can you tell?

Which lines or phrases do you like best? Can you explain why you like them, and how they 'fit' or seem right for the poem?

The Street   *Octavio Paz*
Translated from the Spanish.

Questions to discuss
Read this poem over to yourself and then discuss the following with a partner:
—is the speaker the pursued or the pursuer?
—is he or she expressing fear or loneliness or what?
—which is the poem most like: music, film, cartoon, theatre or a photograph? Why?

If you are studying another language, you might like to try translating a short poem from that language into English. If you can't find a poem yourself, ask your Language teacher or your English teacher to supply you with one. If more than one of you attempts the translation, you will find it interesting to compare translations and to discuss which version comes closest to the meaning of the original. You will find that as you work on the translation, several kinds of problem emerge that will make you think hard about language and about the work you are translating: remember that you are not only translating the words themselves, but aiming to convey in another language the mood, feeling and tone, as well as the rhythms of the original. The results might well be worth publishing in your school magazine.

This poem also lends itself to further exploration in role-play and perhaps even in a drama studio or theatre. It could form part of the narration at the beginning, in the middle, or at the end of a scene or scenes based on the relationship between the pursued and the pursuer.

Because   *James McAuley*

'fecklessness': 'feckless' means worthless, not thinking about the future

'switching': a kind of rattling, swishing sound

'cyst': a small, hollow growth in the body

'call the dead collect': to make a 'collect' call is to reverse the charges

Questions for written answers

1   What is the difference in character between the poet's mother and father?

2   Which of the two do you think the poet is most concerned about? Give evidence.

3   Why 'should this matter to (him) now as much'? Why is he writing the poem?

4   Why is the poem entitled 'Because'?

5   What do lines 3 and 4 suggest about his parents' love for each other?

6   What do the lines 'Once they stood/Tall in my childhood as the school, the steeple' suggest about his parents then and now?

7   How do the rhyme scheme and the form of the poem help convey its meaning and feeling?

Brooklyn Cop   *Norman MacCaig*

'Brooklyn': one of the five boroughs of New York City, and one of the toughest

'hieroglyphs': pictures used for writing by the ancient Egyptians, suggesting not only that his eyes are slit-like, but also that they are hard to decipher

Questions to discuss

This and the poems by Hill, Paz, Cavafy and Lawrence have at least one thing in common: what is it?

How effective do you find the simile of the gorilla in depicting the cop?

Bags Of Meat   *Thomas Hardy*
'drover': someone who drives cattle to market
'picter': picture
'crown': five shillings (25p)
'bouse': booze

Questions to discuss
Pick out the words and phrases that suggest the insensitive handling of the cattle by the men at the auction.
What is the attitude of the two auctioneers?
How does Hardy engage our sympathies for the cattle?

What is the effect of the variation between the longer lines which start, as it were, at the left-hand margin and the shorter, indented lines? Why didn't Hardy just write the whole poem with a consistent margin?

One Flesh   *Elizabeth Jennings*
'flotsam': waste materials washed up on a shore

Questions to discuss
Is it a surprise at the end of the poem that it is, in fact, about the poet's father and mother?
Why is time 'a feather/Touching them gently'?
Compare this poem to 'Because' by James McAuley.

What is the effect of the realisation at the end that it is the daughter of this man and woman that is narrating the poem? Would it have been a better poem if someone other than a daughter had narrated it?

Work And Play   *Ted Hughes*
The long lines in the poem are about the swallow, and the shorter, indented ones about 'the holiday people'. Why does Hughes arrange the poem like this? What feeling is conveyed by the length of the lines? How would you read it?
List the images used to describe the swallow. Then list those used to describe the holiday-makers. Examples to get you started are:
—swallow: 'a whiplash swimmer'
—holiday-makers: 'the serpent of cars'
What qualities are suggested by these images? What is Hughes suggesting about each?
What do the 'work' and 'play' of the title refer to? What is Hughes suggesting about 'work' and 'play'?

There are various activities and kinds of writing that might emerge from a reading of this poem:
—prepare a reading of it in pairs or in larger groups. How are you going to split it into parts, and what tone of voice will you use for various parts of the poem?

—use it as the basis for some improvisation on holiday-makers and the problems they might face before, during or after a holiday.

—use the poem as a model for your own writing about a contrast between two related ideas, like 'Summer and Winter', 'Day and Night', 'Peace and War'; you will have to take a viewpoint, as does Hughes, before you choose your imagery for the poem.

—write an essay entitled 'Work and Play' in which you discuss the generally accepted meanings and associations of those words, and state whether you agree with them.

—write an essay on the poem, discussing how the imagery Hughes chooses determines the 'feel' of the poem, and the strong suggestions that come across.

The Potato Patch   *E. A. Markham*

Questions to discuss
What do you think the island in line 3 represents for Maureen?

Write the letter Maureen might have written home, once she had settled into this new flat.

Night Rain   *John Pepper Clark*
'ardour': passion
'deploying': arranging for action

Questions to discuss
Why 'drumming'?
How is the experience connected to the sea?

Write an account, in diary form, of the poet's experience during this night of rain. Or you may wish to compare this poem with 'It Rains' by Edward Thomas, also from this section.

Holidays In Childhood   *Clifford Dyment*

Questions to discuss
Despite the suggestion that things are 'all just the same' in the second stanza, we know from the last line that 'Harold is dead'. Is there a difference between the yacht as described in the first stanza and as described in the second?

What is the effect of leaving the revelation about Harold's death until the last line? How does it relate to the title of the poem?

Opposition   *Kaneko Mitsuharu*

'scruple': conscience
'hakama': a wide skirt of thick silk, worn by men on formal occasions in Japan

Section 2

Imagery

Double Marlon
Andy Warhol

'*I* see what you mean', we say, or 'I *look* forward to my birthday', comparing the actions of the mind with those of the eyes. We often speak like this, and when we want to explain an idea or process we often make visual references: 'they make things *clear*', we say, as if we were talking about the distinctness of physical shape or colour.

It is through imagery, or pictures, that the world enters our heads. Though we manage to understand abstract ideas like friendship or lateness or hard work, it seems that we must constantly refresh them and keep them alive with particular examples. So a character in John Webster's play, *The Duchess of Malfi*, explaining how he prospers in time of hardship, says 'Blackbirds fatten best in hard weather'. He uses an image. Our minds, in fact, are store-houses of images, pictures of all the things we have ever encountered—blackbirds, bulldogs, Volkswagens, socks, the sea, noses, computers; and it is through the names for them that the world enters poetry.

Imagery may consist of a single word, the mere mention of blackbirds. Or it may be worked out in some detail: as a scene, for example, in which the poet and Governor Brown of California shoot arrows at hay bales, or as a scientifically accurate description of a flower's characteristics, 'fast fading violets covered up in leaves' (Keats, 'Ode To A Nightingale'). To complicate matters, images (in spite of their name) need not be visual only: when Lawrence refers to 'echoes of footsteps' he uses an image that appeals not to the sense of sight but to that of the ear. It is like a heard picture. And it is possible, also, to use imagery of touch, smell and taste. In poetry, the image may derive from any of the senses.

Thus Edward Herbert, in the seventeenth century, wrote the following epitaph on 'a stinking poet':

'Here stinks a poet, I confess,
Yet wanting* breath stinks so much
    less.'
                              *wanting: lacking

Herbert makes a pun on our slang use of a word ('as a poet, he stinks') and our literal use of it ('as a dead body, he stinks'). By playing thus with the imagery of smell, he manages to frame a really ingenious insult.

Not all poetry, however, consists of imagery. The strength of a line may rather be in its sound, as for example where T. S. Eliot in *The Waste Land* repeats the closing-time call from the pubs, 'HURRY UP PLEASE IT'S TIME', again and again like the refrain in a song, until it seems to mean that it is indeed 'time' for all of us, in a most sinister way, the end of the road, the end of our resources. This is hardly an image. Or a poem might consist of abstract statements, though it rarely does, since we are creatures who live most immediately through our senses, particularly through the visual.

In fact, many a poem's power is to be found in the vividness and precision of its imagery. We read of Allen Ginsberg as a child standing on a toilet-seat to be dabbed with calomine lotion for poison ivy (in 'Aunt Rose') or of Thomas Hardy (in 'The Voice') recalling his dead wife in her 'original air-blue gown'. And we say to ourselves, 'Yes, I see.'

THOM GUNN

The Geranium

When I put her out, once, by the garbage pail,
She looked so limp and bedraggled,
So foolish and trusting, like a sick poodle,
Or a wizened aster in late September,
I brought her back in again
For a new routine—
Vitamins, water, and whatever
Sustenance seemed sensible
At the time: she'd lived
So long on gin, bobbie pins, half-smoked cigars, dead beer,　　　*10*
Her shrivelled petals falling
On the faded carpet the stale
Steak grease stuck to her fuzzy leaves.
(Dried-out, she creaked like a tulip.)

The things she endured!
The dumb dames shrieking half the night
Or the two of us, alone, both seedy,
Me breathing booze at her,
She leaning out of her pot toward the window.

Near the end, she seemed almost to hear me—　　　*20*
And that was scary—

So when that snuffling cretin of a maid
Threw her, pot and all, into the trash-can,
I said nothing.

But I sacked the presumptuous hag the next week,
I was that lonely.

Theodore Roethke

Red Wheelbarrow

So much depends
upon

a red wheel
barrow

glazed with rain
water

beside the white
chickens.

William Carlos Williams

Naming Of Parts

Today we have naming of parts. Yesterday,
We had daily cleaning. And tomorrow morning,
We shall have what to do after firing. But today,
Today we have naming of parts. Japonica
Glistens like coral in all of the neighbouring gardens,
    And today we have naming of parts.

This is the lower sling swivel. And this
Is the upper sling swivel, whose use you will see,
When you are given your slings. And this is the piling swivel,
Which in your case you have not got. The branches   *10*
Hold in the gardens their silent, eloquent gestures,
    Which in our case we have not got.

This is the safety-catch, which is always released
With an easy flick of the thumb. And please do not let me
See anyone using his finger. You can do it quite easy
If you have any strength in your thumb. The blossoms
Are fragile and motionless, never letting anyone see
    Any of them using their finger.

And this you can see is the bolt. The purpose of this
Is to open the breech, as you see. We can slide it   *20*
Rapidly backwards and forwards: we call this
Easing the spring. And rapidly backwards and forwards
The early bees are assaulting and fumbling the flowers:
    They call it easing the Spring.

They call it easing the Spring: it is perfectly easy
If you have any strength in your thumb: like the bolt,
And the breech, and the cocking-piece, and the point of balance,
Which in our case we have not got; and the almond-blossom
Silent in all of the gardens and the bees going backwards and
  forwards,   *30*
    For today we have naming of parts.

Henry Reed

Four Glimpses Of Night

1

Eagerly
Like a woman hurrying to her lover
Night comes to the room of the world
And lies, yielding and content
Against the cool round face
Of the moon.

2

Night is a curious child, wandering
Between earth and sky, creeping
In windows and doors, daubing
The entire neighborhood   *10*
With purple paint.
Day
Is an apologetic mother
Cloth in hand
Following after.

3

Peddling
From door to door
Night sells
Black bags of peppermint stars
Heaping cones of vanilla moon   *20*
Until
His wares are gone
Then shuffles homeward
Jingling the gray coins
Of daybreak.

4

Night's brittle song, silver-thin,
Shatters into a billion fragments
Of quiet shadows
At the blaring jazz
Of a morning sun.   *30*

Frank Marshall Davis

she being Brand

she being Brand

-new;and you
know consequently a
little stiff i was
careful of her and(having

thoroughly oiled the universal
joint tested my gas felt of
her radiator made sure her springs were O.

K.)i went right to it flooded-the-carburetor cranked her

up,slipped the   10
clutch(and then somehow got into reverse she
kicked what
the hell)next
minute i was back in neutral tried and

again slo-wly;bare,ly nudg.   ing(my

lev-er Right-
oh and her gears being in
A I shape passed
from low through
second-in-to-high like   20
greasedlightning)just as we turned the corner of Divinity

avenue i touched the accelerator and give

her the juice,good

                (it
was the first ride and believe i we was
happy to see how nice she acted right up to
the last minute coming back down by the Public
Gardens i slammed on
the
internalexpanding   30
&

externalcontracting
brakes Bothatonce and

brought allofher tremB
-ling
to a:dead.

stand-
;Still)

e e cummings

Selling Watermelons

Moscow is milling with watermelons.
Everything breathes a boundless freedom.
And it blows with unbridled fierceness
from the breathless melonvendors.

Stalls. Din. Girls' headscarves.
They laugh. Change bangs down. Knives—

and a choice sample slice.
—Take one, chief, for a long life!

Who's for a melon?
Freshly split!—   *10*
And just as tasty and just as juicy are
the capbands of policemen
and the ranks of motor-scooters.
The September air is fresh and keen
and resonant as a watermelon.

And just as joyfully on its own tack
as the city-limit melon-multitudes,
the earth swings
in its great string bag
of meridians and latitudes!   *20*

Andrei Voznesensky
Translated by Edwin Morgan

The River In March

Now the river is rich, but her voice is low.
It is her Mighty Majesty the sea
Travelling among the villages incognito.

Now the river is poor. No song, just a thin mad whisper.
The winter floods have ruined her.
She squats between draggled banks, fingering her rags and rubbish.

And now the river is rich. A deep choir.
It is the lofty clouds, that work in heaven,
Going on their holiday to the sea.

The river is poor again. All her bones are showing.   *10*
Through a dry wig of bleached flotsam she peers up ashamed
From her slum of sticks.

Now the river is rich, collecting shawls and minerals.
Rain brought fatness, but she takes ninety-nine percent
Leaving the fields just one percent to survive on.

And now she is poor. Now she is East wind sick.
She huddles in holes and corners. The brassy sun gives her a
  headache.
She has lost all her fish. And she shivers.

But now once more she is rich. She is viewing her lands.
A hoard of king-cups spills from her folds, it blazes, it cannot be
  hidden.   *20*
A salmon, a sow of solid silver,

Bulges to glimpse it.

Ted Hughes

Autumn Rain

The plane leaves
fall black and wet
on the lawn;

the cloud sheaves
in heaven's fields set
droop and are drawn

in falling seeds of rain;
the seed of heaven
on my face

falling—I hear again   10
like echoes even
that softly pace

heaven's muffled floor,
the winds that tread
out all the grain

of tears, the store
harvested
in the sheaves of pain

caught up aloft:
the sheaves of dead   20
men that are slain

now winnowed soft
on the floor of heaven;
manna invisible

of all the pain
here to us given;
finely divisible
falling as rain.

D. H. Lawrence

Preludes

I

The winter evening settles down
With smell of steaks in passageways.
Six o'clock.
The burnt-out ends of smoky days.
And now a gusty shower wraps
The grimy scraps
Of withered leaves about your feet
And newspapers from vacant lots;
The showers beat
On broken blinds and chimney-pots,   *10*
And at the corner of the street
A lonely cab-horse steams and stamps.

And then the lighting of the lamps.

II

The morning comes to consciousness
Of faint stale smells of beer
From the sawdust-trampled street
With all its muddy feet that press
To early coffee-stands.

With the other masquerades
That time resumes,
One thinks of all the hands
That are raising dingy shades
In a thousand furnished rooms.   *10*

III

You tossed a blanket from the bed,
You lay upon your back, and waited;
You dozed, and watched the night revealing
The thousand sordid images
Of which your soul was consituted;
They flickered against the ceiling.
And when all the world came back
And the light crept up between the shutters

36

And you heard the sparrows in the gutters,
You had such a vision of the street   *10*
As the street hardly understands;
Sitting along the bed's edge, where
You curled the papers from your hair,
Or clasped the yellow soles of feet
In the palms of both soiled hands.

IV

His soul stretched tight across the skies
That fade behind a city block,
Or trampled by insistent feet
At four and five and six o'clock;
And short square fingers stuffing pipes,
And evening newspapers, and eyes
Assured of certain certainties,
The conscience of a blackened street
Impatient to assume the world.

I am moved by fancies that are curled   *10*
Around these images, and cling:
The notion of some infinitely gentle
Infinitely suffering thing.

Wipe your hand across your mouth, and laugh;
The worlds revolve like ancient women
Gathering fuel in vacant lots.

T. S. Eliot

'He Shot Arrows, But Not At Birds Perching'

Lun yü, VII, 26

The Governor came to visit in the mountains
    we cleaned the house and raked the yard that day.
He'd been east and hadn't slept much
    so napped all afternoon back in the shade.

Young trees and chickens must be tended
    I sprayed apples, and took water to the hens.
Next day we read the papers, spoke of farming,
    of oil, and what would happen to the cars.

And then beside the pond we started laughing,
    got the quiver and bow and strung the bow.   *10*
Arrow after arrow flashing
    hissing under pines in summer breeze

Striking deep in straw bales by the barn.

Gary Snyder

Late Summer

The pumpkin tendrils creep
Along the station platform.
A ladybird peeps
From a chink in the half-closed flowers.

A stopping train comes in.
No one gets on, or off.

On the millet stalk
Growing by the railing
The young ticket-man
Rests his clippers.

Kinoshita Yuji

Europa

Boots and boats—in our bright orange gear
we were such an old-fashioned earthly lot
it seemed almost out of time-phase. We learned
or re-learned how to skate and ski, use snowshoes,
fish through ice-holes though not for fish. Soundings
and samples were our prey. We'd never grade
in years, far less in weeks, the infinite
play and glitter of watery Europa,
waters of crust ice, waters of deep ice,
waters of slush, of warm subcrustal springs,   10
waters of vapour, waters of water.
One day, and only one, we drilled right down
to something solid and so solid-hard
the drill-head screamed into the microphone
and broke, the film showed streaks of metal shards
whizzing across a band of basalt or
glimmery antediluvian turtle-shell
or cast-off titan miner's helmet or—
it must have been the metal scream that roused
our thought and fear and half desire we might   20
have had a living scream returned. Lightly
it sleeps, the imagination. On that smooth moon
men would be driven mad with many dreams,
hissing along the hill-less shining wastes,
or hearing the boat's engine chug the dark
apart, as if a curtain could be drawn
to let the living see even the dead
if they had once had life, if not that life.

Edwin Morgan

Adventures Of Isabel

Isabel met an enormous bear,
Isabel, Isabel, didn't care;
The bear was hungry, the bear was ravenous,
The bear's big mouth was cruel and cavernous.
The bear said, Isabel, glad to meet you,
How do, Isabel, now I'll eat you!
Isabel, Isabel, didn't worry,
Isabel didn't scream or scurry.
She washed her hands and she straightened her hair up,
Then Isabel quietly ate the bear up.   *10*

Once in a night as black as pitch
Isabel met a wicked old witch.
The witch's face was cross and wrinkled,
The witch's gums with teeth were sprinkled.
Ho ho, Isabel! the old witch crowed,
I'll turn you into an ugly toad!
Isabel, Isabel, didn't worry,
Isabel didn't scream or scurry,
She showed no rage and she showed no rancor,
But she turned the witch into milk and drank her.   *20*

Isabel met a hideous giant,
Isabel continued self-reliant.
The giant was hairy, the giant was horrid,
He had one eye in the middle of his forehead.
Good morning Isabel, the giant said,
I'll grind your bones to make my bread.
Isabel, Isabel, didn't worry,
Isabel didn't scream or scurry,
She nibbled the zwieback that she always fed off,
And when it was gone, she cut the giant's head off.   *30*

Isabel met a troublesome doctor,
He punched and he poked till he really shocked her.
The doctor's talk was of coughs and chills
And the doctor's satchel bulged with pills.
The doctor said unto Isabel,
Swallow this, it will make you well.
Isabel, Isabel, didn't worry,

Isabel didn't scream or scurry,
She took those pills from the pill concocter,
And Isabel calmly cured the doctor.   *40*

Ogden Nash

Palm-Tree

Palm-tree: single-legged giant,
        topping the other trees,
          peering at the firmament—
It longs   to pierce the black cloud-ceiling
        and fly away, away,
          if only it had wings.

The tree   seems to express its wish
        in the tossing of its head:
          its fronds heave and swish—
It thinks,   Maybe my leaves are feathers,   *10*
        and nothing stops me now
          from rising on their flutter.

All day   the fronds on the windblown tree
        soar and flap and shudder
          as though it thinks it can fly,
As though   it wanders in the skies,
        travelling who knows where,
          wheeling past the stars—

And then   as soon as the wind dies down,
        the fronds subside, subside: *20*
          the mind of the tree returns
To earth,   recalls that earth is its mother
        and then it likes once more
          its earthly corner.

Rabindranath Tagore

Darlingford

Blazing tropical sunshine
On a hard, white dusty road
That curves round and round
Following the craggy coastline;
Coconut trees fringing the coast,
Thousands and thousands
Of beautiful coconut trees,
Their green and brown arms
Reaching out in all directions—
Reaching up to high heaven   *10*
And sparkling in the sunshine.
Sea coast, rocky sea coast,
Rocky palm-fringed coastline;
Brown-black rocks,
White sea-foam spraying the rocks;
Waves, sparkling waves
Dancing merrily with the breeze;
The incessant song
Of the mighty sea,
A white sail—far out   *20*
Far, far out at sea;
A tiny sailing boat—
White sails all glittering
Flirting with the bright rays
Of the soon setting sun,
Trying to escape their kisses,
In vain—and the jealous winds
Waft her on, on, out to sea
Till sunset; then weary
Of their battle with the sun   *30*
The tired winds
Fold themselves to sleep
And the noble craft
No longer idolized
By her two violent lovers
Drifts slowly into port
In the pale moonlight;
Gone are the violent caresses
Of the sun and restless winds—
She nestles in the cool embrace   *40*

Of quiet waves
And tender moonlight
Southern silvery moonlight
Shining from a pale heaven
Upon a hard, white, dusty road
That curves round and round
Following the craggy coastline
Of Jamaica's southern shore.

Una Marson

Not Waving But Drowning

Nobody heard him, the dead man,
But still he lay moaning:
I was much further out than you thought
And not waving but drowning.

Poor chap, he always loved larking
And now he's dead
It must have been too cold for him his heart gave way,
They said.

Oh, no no no no, it was too cold always
(Still the dead one lay moaning)   *10*
I was much too far out all my life
And not waving but drowning.

Stevie Smith

Cardiac Arrest

This is the time when the gods come
for your heart.
Down the long blue corridors,
past one door, then another,
a last dark turn and then—
light. Simplicity of motion,
of gestures, in a gallery
of white shadows.
And you dream without sleeping:
of miners who scrape coal   10
from the earth like roe from a fish;
of the monks in Hell
with the lead-lined cloaks;
of obsidian eels at a hundred fathoms
who have witnessed the birth of whales;
of the hands against a golden light
which bathed and combed you
and turned you in your sleep.
You are flat on the sidewalk
of a busy city street   20
and a crowd has gathered to watch
the policeman loosen your collar.
High, high in the sunlight
a construction crane raises a man
in a cage—a deus ex machina
swaying against the clouds.
Truly, the man could be a god,
rising even higher now, escaping
with your heartbeat in the palm of his hand.

Nicholas Christopher

'That world will come like a thief'

That world will come like a thief
and steal all we possess
Poor and naked, we will be transparent as glass
that both cuts and reflects.

Karol Wojtyla

'And the days are not full enough'

And the days are not full enough
And the nights are not full enough
And life slips by like a field mouse
              Not shaking the grass.

Ezra Pound

Desire

Like a Bacon's
itch for Eggs
and the Bread's
need for Butter

Like the Fish's
fancy for Chips
and a Hamburger's
hunger for Ketchup

Like a Whisky's
yen for Soda
and the Rum's
penchant for Cola

10

Like the Pen's
lust for Paper
and a Bullet's
thirst for Blood

My Desire for You.

Cecil Rajendra

Notes and activities

The Geranium   *Theodore Roethke*
'aster' (line 4): a white or light blue flower
'bobbie-pin' (line 10): a hair-grip

Questions to discuss
Why does the poet refer to the geranium as 'she'? Is the woman to whom the geranium is compared more like a wife, a mother or a daughter—or a combination of all three?
What does the account of the geranium tell us about the poet's own life?
Why is this flower, which would be inexpensive to replace, so important to the writer?

Write about your impressions of the speaker, making it clear how they arise from the language of the poem.

Red Wheelbarrow   *William Carlos Williams*
It is important to read this poem, as any other, being aware of how it has been printed on the page. It is not written as a sentence in prose. Try rewriting the poem, or cutting it up in different ways. Notice how Williams has made the poem hard to read:
> 'a red wheel
> barrow'
is not as easy to take in as 'a red wheelbarrow'.

Questions to discuss
'So much depends . . . ' but Williams does not say what it is that does depend. Is he suggesting that what is important is that we observe everyday, ordinary objects with the care and attention that he devotes to the red wheelbarrow?

Write some brief descriptions of familiar objects. Experiment with cutting up the descriptions and reassembling them in different ways. How do the different arrangements affect the descriptions?

Naming Of Parts   *Henry Reed*
This poem must be read aloud; but, before it is, one should consider whether it might be best read by one voice or two. The poem was written during the Second World War. Who is teaching the naming of parts and who is learning? Which lines might be spoken by which character?

Questions to discuss
Each stanza contains a comparison between what the first speaker says and what the second speaker notices. Discuss what the comparison is in each stanza and how that comparison is presented.

What is the second speaker paying attention to in each stanza? Does this suggest anything about his attitude to war?

How can the branches be both 'silent' and 'eloquent' (lines 10–11)?

What effect is created by the repetition of words and phrases within each stanza?

Write about your impressions of the two speakers. What words or phrases suggest these impressions?

Write about the poem. You may wish to consider the following:

—any phrases, lines or ideas that you feel are interesting

—how the ones you have selected have helped to convey the feeling of the poem or have helped you to understand what the poet is trying to express

—your views about the way the poet has expressed himself.

Four Glimpses Of Night   *Frank Marshall Davis*

Questions to discuss

To what is night compared in each of the four sections?

To what is day compared in sections 2, 3 and 4?

What do these comparisons suggest about Davis's feelings about, and attitude towards, night and day?

Are 'black bags of peppermint stars' and 'heaping cones of vanilla moons' attractive images? How do they affect our view of night in this poem? With what, in this stanza, do these images contrast and to what effect?

Write your own poem, 'Four Glimpses', about night and day, or about anyone or anything that interests you; you might even write about four glimpses of yourself.

she being Brand   *e e cummings*

Questions to discuss

This poem is an extended metaphor. At what point do we realise exactly what the poem is about?

Is the poem simply clever or is cummings making a point about men's attitude to women? (Is the 'i' in the poem cummings himself?)

cummings' poems are always laid out in an interesting way. Are there any parts of the layout which seem to you effective in that they aid or reflect the meaning? For example, why, in line 15, is 'slowly' written as 'slo-wly'? Or why, in line 33, is 'both at once' written as 'Bothatonce'?

Write about anything in the poem that interests you. This may include words, phrases, striking images, a feeling, an attitude or the character of the speaker—or anything else that has struck you.

Selling Watermelons   *Andrei Voznesensky translated by*
   Edwin Morgan

Questions to discuss

This poem is an exciting, dramatic portrait of a Moscow street scene—notice the alliterative 'm' and 'b' sounds enlivening the first four lines, the lively detail of lines 5 and 6, the dramatic speech of lines 8–10—until the final simile in lines 16–20. To what is the earth being compared here? What does this comparison, bearing in mind the first fifteen lines, suggest about life on earth? Is this comparison too fanciful or does it work visually (can you visualise it?)— how does it make you visualise the earth? Do lines 14–15 prepare us in any way for this comparison?

Write about the poem in any way that seems interesting to you. You may like to consider the following topics as guides:
—the dramatic nature and situation of the poem
—interesting and effective use of language
—the poet's attitude to life.

The River In March   *Ted Hughes*

'incognito' (line 3): concealing one's identity
'flotsam' (line 11): things lost at sea and found floating on it
'king-cups' (line 20): buttercups
'sow' (line 21): a channel for leading molten metal to the moulds in casting pig iron—note the shape of such a channel

Questions to discuss
This poem is based on a series of contrasts. What impression of the river do these contrasts give?
Examine the poem stanza by stanza. See what examples of personification you can find. To what is the river metaphorically compared in each stanza? Do these metaphors affect the way we see the river? How?
What image in the first four lines especially creates an impression of riches and how is this phrase given emphasis?

Write about the way Hughes presents the river—the people he imagines the river to be—making it clear whether or not you feel his images and use of language are interesting and effective.

Autumn Rain   *D. H. Lawrence*

'plane' (line 1): a tree
'manna' (line 24): food from heaven
To produce crops, seeds are planted which are harvested when fully grown. The results may be bound in sheaves which are then trodden out to produce the grain, which is what is wanted. What is unwanted, the stalks, remain in sheaves which can be thrown away.

Questions to discuss
To what does Lawrence compare the clouds in stanza 2?
To what does Lawrence compare the rain in stanza 3?
To what is heaven compared in stanza 5?
To what is the rain compared in the final stanza?

Write about the metaphor which Lawrence uses in this poem. Try to show how it is developed from the simple description of the first three lines and say whether or not you think it is effective or too fanciful.

Preludes *T. S. Eliot*

'Preludes' is a group of four poems which have two things in common: they are all set in the city, against an urban background, and they all evoke a similar mood. The title is taken from a set of piano pieces by Chopin which are also intended to evoke a mood.

'vacant lots' (I, line 8): empty pieces of land in a city, where vagrants often make fires

'masquerades' (II, line 6): a pretence, an empty show

'furnished rooms' (II, line 10): in a city, furnished rooms are usually cheap and dirty. If one rents one of these, one can expect to have to share a bathroom and a kitchen with the other tenants. Why might it be more depressing to rent a room that is furnished as opposed to one that is unfurnished?

'conscience' (IV, line 8): consciousness

'assume' (IV, line 9): to take control of, to take over

Questions to discuss

This is a poem which seems difficult at first, as there is no story line holding the poem together. As we have said, this poem creates a mood rather than telling a story. You may wish to discuss the following questions in pairs or groups before attempting to come to a decision as a class:

Section I

After a careful reading of the whole poem, write down all the adjectives in section I; there are nine of them. Taken together, what mood do they suggest?

Explain the comparison in line 4; what does it suggest?

What has happened to the natural world in the city environment of the poem?

Section II

What mood is suggested to you by the first two lines?

What effect does the city seem to have on the people? Why are they referred to as 'feet' and 'hands' rather than as whole human beings?

What is suggested about city life by the word 'masquerade'?

What does the word 'thousand' add to our view of the city?

What adjectives in this section add to the impression given by the adjectives in the first section?

Section III

Here we are presented with a picture, or an image, of a woman. What is suggested about her by lines 4 and 5?

What is suggested to you by lines 10 and 11?

The final two lines of this section reveal that the woman is dirty; is there any difference between her 'yellow' feet and her 'soiled' hands?

Section IV

Here we are presented initially with the image of man. The first line is hard, if not impossible, to picture; but what do the words, especially 'stretched tight', suggest?

How does the rhythm in line 4 echo the meaning of the line?

In what way might a street 'assume' the rest of the world?

How do Eliot's feelings change in lines 10–13?

How do they change again in line 14?

What mood is suggested to you by this image?

What feelings are suggested by the final simile?

Suggestions for writing

If you feel you have answered most of these questions, read the poem again to yourself before hearing it read aloud; then write about the poem, attempting to say what Eliot's view of city life is and how he presents it.

'He Shot Arrows But Not At Birds Perching' *Gary Snyder*

Questions to discuss

What attitude to life is expressed in the first 8 lines?

Why is the final line separate from the rest of the poem?

What does the image in lines 11–13, taken with the title, suggest? Does it contrast in any way with the rest of the poem?

What impression do you gain of the Governor and the speaker of the poem?

Europa *Edwin Morgan*

Europa is a moon of Jupiter and this poem might be described as an example of science fiction writing.

Write about the poem, making it clear, by referring to specific details, what impression you gain of Europa and how you gain that impression. Put yourself in the place of one of the scientists/explorers. Describe your thoughts and feelings as you analyse and explore Europa.

Adventures Of Isabel *Ogden Nash*

'zwieback' (line 29): a hard biscuit

Questions to discuss

What images and rhymes add to the fun of this poem?

What details in the poem strike you as being those of a children's story?

What details strike you as being inappropriate to a children's story? Why?

What is the overall effect of this poem?

Palm-Tree *Rabindranath Tagore*

'firmament': the sky, the heavens

'fronds': leaves, branches

Questions to discuss

What is the effect of the arrangement of the words in this poem?

What is the principal image with which the palm-tree is compared?

Darlingford *Una Marson*

Write an appreciation of a place you love, either in verse or in prose.

Not Waving But Drowning *Stevie Smith*

Questions to discuss
Explain the situation of the poem.
What impression has Smith created by running two sentences together in line 17? Is the image that dominates this poem effective—does it succeed visually and as an idea?
What can you say about the structure of this poem?

Cardiac Arrest *Nicholas Christopher*

Title: a heart attack
'obsidian' (line 14): a dark, volcanic rock
'deus ex machina' (line 25): literally means a god from a machine. It is used to mean an unlikely device, introduced into a play or a novel, to resolve the plot.

Questions to discuss
What is suggested about the sick man by the images in the first 18 lines?
What is suggested about the sick man by the final image?
What effect does the poet create by not explaining the situation of the poem until lines 19–22?
Does the poem suggest anything about mankind in general?

'That world will come like a thief ...' *Karol Wojtyla*

Karol Wojtyla is Pope John Paul II.

Questions to discuss
In a small group, discuss the meaning of the poem. In particular, ask yourselves:
—Why is the world described as 'like a thief'?
—Why 'that world'?
—What does 'naked' suggest about us?
—Why 'Transparent as glass ...'?
—Why 'that both cuts and reflects'?

'And the days are not full enough' *Ezra Pound*

Questions to discuss
What feeling, mood or impression does Pound create by beginning each of the first three lines with 'and'?
What does 'Not shaking the grass' suggest about the field mouse?
What does the simile in lines 3–4 suggest about Pound's feelings towards the way we live our lives?
Would the poem be as effective without the first two lines? What do they add?

51

Section 3

Political

Communist and Socialist

R. B. Kitaj

*P*oetry and politics don't mix. Poetry is not propaganda. Poetry never has a message. Political speeches come out of arguments with other people and aim to shape opinion. But poetry shapes no opinions, it issues only from a writer's quarrel with him or herself.

These are common views of the nature of poetry and they have been influential in making many people believe that political poetry isn't really poetry at all. Political poetry, it is suggested, is just slogan-mongering. It is always top-heavy with opinions.

This 'aesthetic' view of poetry is usually the expression of a privileged and dominant social and/or cultural position. Writers who belong to oppressed or marginalised cultures recognise that the very act of writing or reciting poems at public readings is political. It isn't necessarily a matter of choosing a political subject—the writer who chooses, for example, to write in non-standard English is making a political statement by selecting certain words and rhythms, and rejecting others.

In Britain many literary critics have chosen to ignore political issues and have argued that poems 'transcend' history and politics. Howevever, the greatest English non-dramatic poet—John Milton—was a committed political writer. He was a radical republican who supported the English revolution and wrote pamphlets in support of it. His greatest poem, *Paradise Lost,* analyses the failure of the revolution and looks forward to another revolution in the future which will finally overthrow monarchy and superstition. Another great English seventeenth century poet, John Dryden, at first supported Cromwell, the Lord Protector of the new revolutionary state, but after the restoration of the monarchy he became a committed monarchist and conservative. His masterpiece, *Absalom and Achitophel,* is a defence of Charles II and an attack on Charles' enemies, many of whom were republicans.

Perhaps all poetry either supports the state or dissents from it. In a sense all poetry is political. We should not make an artificial division between the writer who creates works of art and the citizen who is taxed or conscripted or arrested by the forces of the state he or she belongs to.

TOM PAULIN

53

The Honourable Company

He said, 'It was our custom at the time
To join the Honourable Company of Straight-Shooters.
Finding myself in the firing squad,
I naturally aimed straight.

Among the prisoners who would reserve
Their final diatribes for these occasions,
Was a young man questioning our values
Convicted for treason.

He paid the normal price, and cleaning our rifles
We turned our thoughts to what the peace might bring;   *10*
Of course there were many young men then
Questioning our values.

It is not his innocence that still disturbs me,
Nor his gesticulation and manner. It is
That having been young myself,
I recall no subversion.

On my part. As I have said, it was our custom
To join the Honourable Company of Sharp-Shooters.
Finding myself in the firing squad,
I naturally aimed straight.'   *20*

Peter Champkin

English Scene

You sit at a table with two other men

Your left wrist slants in front of your throat
Your right incisors chew the nail on your left little finger
Your right index fingernail ploughs across the grain of the tabletop

You are nervous, obviously

You are right to be nervous, obviously

The man on one side of you has less money than you
He wants your money

The man on the other side of you has more money than you
He wants your money

Your left arm protects your throat
They usually go for the throat

Adrian Mitchell

I'm Explaining A Few Things

You are going to ask: and where are the lilacs?
and the poppy-petalled metaphysics?
and the rain repeatedly spattering
its words and drilling them full
of apertures and birds?

I'll tell you all the news.

I lived in a suburb,
a suburb of Madrid, with bells,
and clocks, and trees.

From there you could look out   *10*
over Castille's dry face:
a leather ocean.
                    My house was called
the house of flowers, because in every cranny
geraniums burst: it was
a good-looking house
with its dogs and children.
                              Remember, Raúl?
Eh, Rafael?
              Federico, do you remember   *20*
from under the ground
where the light of June drowned flowers in your mouth?
                                        Brother, my brother!

Everything
loud with big voices, the salt of merchandises,
pile-ups of palpitating bread,
the stalls of my suburb of Argüelles with its statue
like a drained inkwell in a swirl of hake:
oil flowed into spoons,
a deep baying   *30*
of feet and hands swelled in the streets;
metres, litres, the sharp
measure of life,
                    stacked-up fish,
the texture of roofs with a cold sun in which
the weather vane falters,
the fine, frenzied ivory of potatoes,
wave on wave of tomatoes rolling down to the sea.

And one morning all that was burning,
one morning the bonfires   *40*
leapt out of the earth
devouring human beings—
and from then on fire,
gunpowder from then on,
and from then on blood.

Bandits with planes and Moors,
bandits with finger-rings and duchesses,
bandits with black friars spattering blessings
came through the sky to kill children
and the blood of children ran through the streets   *50*
without fuss, like children's blood.

Jackals that the jackals would despise,
stones that the dry thistle would bite on and spit out,
vipers that the vipers would abominate!

Face to face with you I have seen the blood
of Spain tower like a tide
to drown you in one wave
of pride and knives!

Treacherous
generals: *60*
see my dead house,
look at broken Spain:

from every house burning metal flows
instead of flowers,
from every socket of Spain
Spain emerges
and from every dead child a rifle with eyes,
and from every crime bullets are born
which will one day find
the bull's eye of your hearts.   *70*

And you will ask: why doesn't his poetry
speak of dreams and leaves
and the great volcanoes of his native land?
Come and see the blood in the streets.
Come and see
the blood in the streets.
Come and see the blood
in the streets!

Pablo Neruda

Listen To Me

If you want to speak
your punishment is death.
If you want to breathe
your place is in the prison.
If you want to walk
then cut off your legs
and carry them in your arms.
If you want to laugh
hang upside down in a well.
If you want to think   *10*
then shut all the doors
and throw away the key.
If you want to cry
then sink into the river.
If you want to live
then become a cobweb on the cave
of your dreams.
And if you want to forget everything
then pause and think:
of the word you first learnt.

Kishwar Naheed

Brief Thoughts On Exactness

Fish
    move exactly there and exactly then,
just as
    birds have their inbuilt exact measure of time and place.

But mankind,
    deprived of instinct, is aided
    by scientific research, the essence of which
    this story shows.

A certain soldier
    had to fire a gun every evening exactly at six.   *10*
    He did it like a soldier. When his exactness
    was checked, he stated:

I follow
    an absolutely precise chronometer in the shop-window
    of the clockmaker downtown. Every day at seventeen
    forty-five I set my watch by it and
    proceed up the hill where the gun stands ready.
    At seventeen fifty-nine exactly I reach the gun
    and exactly at eighteen hours I fire.

It was found   *20*
    that this method of firing was absolutely exact.
    There was only the chronometer to be checked.
    The clockmaker downtown was asked about its exactness.

Oh, said the clockmaker,
    this instrument is one of the most exact. Imagine,
    for years a gun has been fired here at six exactly.
    And every day I look at the chronometer
    and it always shows exactly six.

So much for exactness.
    And the fish move in the waters and the heavens are filled *30*
    with the murmur of wings, while

The chronometers tick and the guns thunder.

Miroslav Holub

Waiting For The Barbarians

What are we waiting for, assembled in the forum?

   The barbarians are due here today.

Why isn't anything going on in the senate?
Why are the senators sitting there without legislating?

   Because the barbarians are coming today.
   What's the point of senators making laws now?
   Once the barbarians are here, they'll do the legislating.

Why did our emperor get up so early,
and why is he sitting enthroned at the city's main gate,
in state, wearing the crown?   *10*

   Because the barbarians are coming today
   and the emperor's waiting to receive their leader.
   He's even got a scroll to give him,
   loaded with titles, with imposing names.

Why have our two consuls and praetors come out today
wearing their embroidered, their scarlet togas?
Why have they put on bracelets with so many amethysts,
rings sparkling with magnificent emeralds?
Why are they carrying elegant canes
beautifully worked in silver and gold?   *20*

   Because the barbarians are coming today
   and things like that dazzle the barbarians.

Why don't our distinguished orators turn up as usual
to make their speeches, say what they have to say?

   Because the barbarians are coming today
   and they're bored by rhetoric and public speaking.

Why this sudden bewilderment, this confusion?
(How serious people's faces have become.)
Why are the streets and squares emptying so rapidly,
everyone going home lost in thought?   *30*

   Because night has fallen and the barbarians haven't come.
   And some of our men just in from the border say
   there are no barbarians any longer.

Now what's going to happen to us without barbarians?
They were, those people, a kind of solution.

C. P. Cavafy

Epitaph On A Tyrant

Perfection, of a kind, was what he was after,
And the poetry he invented was easy to understand;
He knew human folly like the back of his hand,
And was greatly interested in armies and fleets;
When he laughed, respectable senators burst with laughter,
And when he cried the little children died in the streets.

W. H. Auden

The Educators

In their
limousines the
teachers come: by
hundreds. O the
square is
blackened with dark suits, with grave
scholastic faces. They
wait to be summoned.
                 These are the
educators, the   *10*
father-figures. O you could
warm with love for the firm lips, the
responsible foreheads. Their
ties are strongly set, between their collars. They
pass with dignity the exasperation of waiting.

A
bell rings. They turn. On the
wide steps my
dwarf is standing, both hands raised. He
cackles with laughter. Welcome, he cries, welcome   *20*
to our elaborate Palace. It is indeed. He
is tumbling in cartwheels over the steps. The
teachers turn to each other their grave faces.

With
a single grab they have him up by the shoulders. They
dismantle him. Limbs, O
limbs and delicate organs, limbs and
guts, eyes, the tongue, the
lobes of the brain, glands; tonsils, several
eyes, limbs, the tongue,   *30*
a kidney, pants, livers, more
kidneys, limbs, the tongue
pass from hand to hand, in their serious hands. He is
utterly gone. Wide
crumbling steps.

They
return to their cars. They
drive off smoothly, without disorder;
watching the road.

D. M. Black

I Saw A Jolly Hunter

I saw a jolly hunter
    With a jolly gun
Walking in the country
    In the jolly sun.

In the jolly meadow
    Sat a jolly hare.
Saw the jolly hunter.
    Took jolly care.

Hunter jolly eager—
    Sight of jolly prey.   10
Forgot gun pointing
    Wrong jolly way.

Jolly hunter jolly head
    Over heels gone.
Jolly old safety catch
    Not jolly on.

Bang went the jolly gun
    Hunter jolly dead.
Jolly hare got clean away
    Jolly good, I said.

Charles Causley

Hawk Roosting

I sit in the top of the wood, my eyes closed.
Inaction, no falsifying dream
Between my hooked head and hooked feet:
Or in sleep rehearse perfect kills and eat.

The convenience of the high trees!
The air's buoyancy and the sun's ray
Are of advantage to me;
And the earth's face upward for my inspection.

My feet are locked upon the rough bark.
It took the whole of Creation   10
To produce my foot, my each feather:
Now I hold Creation in my foot

Or fly up, and revolve it all slowly—
I kill where I please because it is all mine.
There is no sophistry in my body:
My manners are tearing off heads—

The allotment of death.
For the one path of my flight is direct
Through the bones of the living.
No arguments assert my right: 20

The sun is behind me.
Nothing has changed since I began.
My eye has permitted no change.
I am going to keep things like this.

Ted Hughes

Everything New Is Better Than Everything Old

How do I know, comrade
That a house built today
Has a purpose and is being used?
And that the brand new constructions
Which clash with the rest of the street and
Whose intent I don't know
Are such a revelation to me?

Because I know:
Everything new
Is better than everything old.   *10*

Would you not agree:
A man who puts on a clean shirt
Is a new man?
The woman who had just had a wash
Is a new woman.
New too
At all-night meetings in a smoke-filled room, the speaker
Starting a new speech.
Everything new
Is better than everything old.   *20*

In the incomplete statistics
Uncut books, factory-new machines
I see the reasons why you get up in the mornings.
The men who on a new chart
Draw a new line across a white patch
The comrades who cut the pages of a book
The happy men
Pouring the first oil into a machine
They are the ones who understand:
Everything new
Is better than everything old.   *30*

Bertolt Brecht

The Unknown Citizen

(To JS/07/M/378

This Marble Monument Is Erected By The State)

He was found by the Bureau of Statistics to be
One against whom there was no official complaint,
And all the reports on his conduct agree
That, in the modern sense of an old-fashioned word, he was a saint,
For in everything he did he served the Greater Community.
Except for the War till the day he retired
He worked in a factory and never got fired,
But satisfied his employers, Fudge Motors Inc.
Yet he wasn't a scab or odd in his views,
For his Union reports that he paid his dues,   10
(Our report on his Union shows it was sound)
And our Social Psychology workers found
That he was popular with his mates and liked a drink.
The Press are convinced that he bought a paper every day
And that his reactions to advertisements were normal in every way.
Policies taken out in his name prove that he was fully insured,
And his Health-card shows he was once in hospital but left it cured.
Both Producers Research and High-Grade Living declare
He was fully sensible to the advantages of the Instalment Plan
And had everything necessary to the Modern Man,   20
A phonograph, a radio, a car and a frigidaire.
Our researchers into Public Opinion are content
That he held the proper opinions for the time of year;
When there was peace, he was for peace; when there was war, he
  went.
He was married and added five children to the population,
Which our Eugenist says was the right number for a parent of his
  generation,
And our teachers report that he never interfered with their
  education.
Was he free? Was he happy? The question is absurd:
Had anything been wrong, we should certainly have heard.

W. H. Auden

Buy One Now

This is a new sort of Poem,
it is Biological.
It contains a special Ingredient
(Pat. pend.) which makes it different
From other brands of poem on the market.

This new Poem does the work for you.
Just drop your mind into it
And leave it to soak
While you relax with the telly
Or go out to the pub   *10*
Or (if that is what you like)
You read a book.

It does the work for you
While (if that is what you like)
You sleep. For it is Biological
(Pat. pend.), it penetrates
Into the darkest recesses,
It removes the understains
Which it is difficult for us
Even to speak of.   *20*

Its action is so gentle
That the most delicate mind is unharmed.
This new sort of Poem
Contains an exclusive new Ingredient
(Known only to every jackass in the trade)
And can be found in practically any magazine
You care to mention.

D. J. Enright

Common Sense

An agricultural labourer, who has
A wife and four children, receives 20s a week
$\frac{3}{4}$ buys food, and the members of the family
Have three meals a day.
How much is that per person per meal?
        —From Pitman's Common Sense Arithmetic, 1917

A gardener, paid 24s a week, is
Fined $\frac{1}{3}$ if he comes to work late.
At the end of 26 weeks, he receives
£30.5.3. How   10
Often was he late?
        —From Pitman's Common Sense Arithmetic, 1917

A milk dealer buys milk at 3d a quart. He
Dilutes it with 3% water and sells
124 gallons of the mixture at
4d per quart. How much of his profit is made by
Adulterating the milk?
        —From Pitman's Common Sense Arithmetic, 1917

The table printed below gives the number
Of paupers in the United Kingdom, and
The total cost of poor relief.   20
Find the average number
Of paupers per ten thousand people.
        —From Pitman's Common Sense Arithmetic, 1917

An army had to march to the relief of
A besieged town, 500 miles away, which
Had telegraphed that it could hold out for 18 days.
The army made forced marches at the rate of 18
Miles a day. Would it be there in time?
        —From Pitman's Common Sense Arithmetic, 1917   30

Out of an army of 28,000 men,
15% were
Killed, 25% were
Wounded. Calculate
how many men there were left to fight.
        —From Pitman's Common Sense Arithmetic, 1917

These sums are offered to
That host of young people in our Elementary Schools,
  who
Are so ardently desirous of setting   *40*
Foot upon the first rung of the
Educational ladder . . .
  —From Pitman's Common Sense Arithmetic, 1917

Alan Brownjohn

A Consumer's Report

The name of the product I tested is *Life*.
I have completed the form you sent me
and understand that my answers are confidential.

I had it as a gift,
I didn't feel much while using it,
in fact I think I'd have liked to be more excited.
It seemed gentle on the hands
but left an embarrassing deposit behind.
It was not economical
and I have used much more than I thought   *10*
(I suppose I have about half left
but it's difficult to tell)—
Although the instructions are fairly large
there are so many of them
I don't know which to follow, especially
as they seem to contradict each other.
I'm not sure such a thing
should be put in the way of children
it's difficult to think of a purpose
for it. One of my friends says
it's just to keep its maker in a job.   *20*
Also the price is much too high.
Things are piling up so fast,
after all, the world got by
for a thousand million years
without this, do we need it now?
(Incidentally, please ask your man
to stop calling me 'the respondent';
I don't like the sound of it.)
There seem to be a lot of different labels,   *30*
sizes and colours should be uniform,
the shape is awkward, it's waterproof
but not heat resistant, it doesn't keep
yet it's very difficult to get rid of.
Whenever they make it cheaper they seem
to put less in: if you say you don't
want it, then it's delivered anyway—
I'd agree it's a popular product,
it's got into the language; people

even say they're on the side of it.   *40*
Personally I think it's overdone,
a small thing people are ready
to behave badly about. I think
we should take it for granted. If its
experts are called philosophers or market
researchers or historians, we shouldn't
care. We are the consumers and the last
law makers. So finally, I'd buy it.
But the question of a 'best buy'
I'd like to leave until I get   *50*
the competitive product you said you'd send.

Peter Porter

Cleator Moor

From one shaft at Cleator Moor
They mined for coal and iron ore.
This harvest below ground could show
Black and red currants on one tree.

In furnaces they burnt the coal,
The ore was smelted into steel,
And railway lines from end to end
Corseted the bulging land.

Pylons sprouted on the fells,
Stakes were driven in like nails,   *10*
And the ploughed fields of Devonshire
Were sliced with the steel of Cleator Moor.

The land waxed fat and greedy too,
It would not share the fruits it grew,
And coal and ore, as sloe and plum,
Lay black and red for jamming time.

The pylons rusted on the fells,
The gutters leaked beside the walls,
And women searched the ebb-tide tracks
For knobs of coal or broken sticks.   *20*

But now the pits are wick with men,
Digging like dogs dig for a bone:
For food and life *we* dig the earth—
In Cleator Moor they dig for death.

Every wagon of cold coal
Is fire to drive a turbine wheel;
Every knuckle of soft ore
A bullet in a soldier's ear.

The miner at the rockface stands,
With his segged and bleeding hands   *30*
Heaps on his head the fiery coal,
And feels the iron in his soul.

Norman Nicholson

Dulce Et Decorum Est

Bent double, like old beggars under sacks,
Knock-kneed, coughing like hags, we cursed through sludge,
Till on the haunting flares we turned our backs
And towards our distant rest began to trudge.
Men marched asleep. Many had lost their boots
But limped on, blood-shod. All went lame; all blind;
Drunk with fatigue; deaf even to the hoots
Of tired, outstripped Five-Nines that dropped behind.

Gas! Gas! Quick, boys!—An ecstasy of fumbling,
Fitting the clumsy helmets just in time;   10
But someone still was yelling out and stumbling
And floundering like a man in fire or lime . . .
Dim, through the misty panes and thick green light,
As under a green sea, I saw him drowning.

In all my dreams, before my helpless sight,
He plunges at me, guttering, choking, drowning.

If in some smothering dreams you too could pace
Behind the wagon that we flung him in,
And watch the white eyes writhing in his face,
His hanging face, like a devil's sick of sin;   20
If you could hear, at every jolt, the blood
Come gargling from the froth-corrupted lungs,
Obscene as cancer, bitter as the cud
Of vile, incurable sores on innocent tongues,—
My friend, you would not tell with such high zest
To children ardent for some desperate glory,
The old Lie: Dulce et decorum est
Pro patria mori.

Wilfred Owen

73

Military Two-Step

While millions are still in need of basic amenities such as food, shelter, medicare and education, expenditure on arms today has escalated to such a point that for each man, woman and child there is now 3.5 tons of T.N.T.

You say your shack
needs restoration
the roof leaks
the walls crack
it's a rat & cock-
roach abomination.

Now don't you worry
you can always jive
with your 3.5
tons of T.N.T.   10

You say the children
are in dire need
of an education
they're bright & eager
but you can't afford
kindergarten or teacher.

Now don't you worry
you can always jive
with your 3.5
tons of T.N.T.   20

You say the family
is always hungry
there's no food
in the larder
& you have to walk
six scorching miles
for a pail of water.

Now don't you worry
you can always jive
with your 3.5
tons of T.N.T.   30

You say your daughter
died last month
from chronic cholera
she would've been saved
but you couldn't raise
the fees for a doctor.

Now don't you worry
you can always jive
with your 3.5
tons of T.N.T.

Cecil Rajendra

Song Of The Banana Man

Tourist, white man wiping his face,
Met me in Golden Grove market place.
He looked at my old clothes brown with stain
And soaked right through with the Portland rain.
He cast his eye, and turned up his nose
And said, 'You're a beggar man I suppose,'
He said, 'Boy get some occupation,
Be of some value to your nation.'

I said, 'By God and this big right hand
You must recognise a banana man.'   *10*

Up in the hills where the streams are cool,
Where mullet and janga swim in the pool,
I have ten acres of mountain side
And a dainty foot donkey that I ride
Four Gros Michel and four Lacatan
Some coconut trees and some hills of yam
And I pasture on that very same land
Five she goats and a big black ram.

That, by God and this big right hand
Is the property of the banana man.   *20*

I leave my yard early morning time
And set my foot to the mountain climb
I bend my back for the hot-sun toil
And my cutlass rings on the stony soil,
Clearing and weeding, digging and planting,
Till Massa sun drop back a John Crow mountain
Then home again in cool evening time
Perhaps whistling this little rhyme,

Praise God and this big right hand
I will live and die a banana man.   *30*

Banana day is my special day
I cut my stems and I'm on my way
Load up the donkey, leave the land
Head down the hill to banana stand,
When the truck comes down I take a ride

All the way down to the harbour side;
That is the night when you tourist man
Would change your place with a banana man.

Yes, praise God and my big right hand
I will live and die a banana man.   *40*

The bay is calm and the moon is bright
The hills look black though the sky is light
Down at the dock is an English ship
Resting after her ocean trip
While on the pier is a monstrous hustle
Tally men, carriers all in a bustle
With the stems on their heads in a long black snake
Some singing the songs that banana men make.

Like Praise God and my big right hand
I will live and die a banana man.   *50*

Then the payment comes and we have some fun
Me, Zekiel, Breda and Duppy Son
Down at the bar near United wharf,
Knock back a white rum, bus' a laugh
Fill the empty bag for further toil
With saltfish, breadfruit and coconut oil
Then head back home to my yard to sleep
A proper sleep that is long and deep.

Yes, praise God and my big right hand
I will live and die a banana man.   *60*

So when you see these old clothes brown with stain
And soaked clean through with Portland rain
Don't cast your eyes nor turn your nose
Don't judge a man by his patchy clothes
I'm a strong man a proud man and I'm free
Part of these mountains part of this sea
I know myself and I know my ways
And will say with pride to the end of my days,

Praise God and my big right hand
I will live and die a banana man.

Evan Jones   *70*

77

Politics

One day, two men were shipwrecked
  On an Island far away.
They hardly knew each other, so
  There wasn't much to say.

By the time a week had passed,
  The two were rather bored;
And so they went their separate ways
  Each of his own accord.

Yes, separate lives for different men;
  This answer seemed the best.   *10*
One lived on the Eastern side;
  The other, to the West.

After a month, a problem emerged;
  How could they bide their time?
There was nothing here to buy
  And neither had a dime.

So they turned to politics
  (After all, here they were free.)
Each ruled over a herd of baboons
  And governed from a tree.   *20*

One was a Fascist dictator;
  The other, a Democrat.
But both held absolute power
  And did all they could with that.

Four year plans were developed;
  Troops were armed and trained.
(The baboons, by the way, did little but eat
  And they all ran away when it rained.)

Borders were drawn out and settled.
  Pacts were written and signed.   *30*
Trade was begun and a currency too,
  Nuclear bombs were designed.

Everything flourished and went very well,
  But soon the two found it a bore.
They planned a few interesting terrorist attacks
  And said that the answer was war.

The baboons, by this time, had begun to be cross
  And gathered throughout the wood,
Wondering why they were all getting bombed
  For the so-called 'common good'.   *40*

Armed with bananas, they crept up behind
  A major official tree.
At one baboon's shout, the two men stepped out,
  After which both were thrown in the sea.

Once they were wet, they both saw the folly
  Of what they had done out of greed.
But sure enough, one week later,
  Neither had paid any heed.

They swam to another island,
  Vowing that peace was best.   *50*
But nevertheless, one headed for East
  While the other decided on West.

Sarah Goossens

Notes and activities

The Honourable Company   *Peter Champkin*
'Straight Shooters' (line 2): a straight shooter is someone who behaves or thinks conventionally
'subversion' (line 16): an attempt to ruin a government or a person

Questions to discuss
Why is the speaker in the firing squad?
Why does he not refuse to shoot a man?
Why is the man being shot?
What are the tone and effect of the word 'naturally' in the last line?

What impression do you gain from this poem of the speaker, his values and the values of the world in which he is living? What details create this impression?

English Scene   *Adrian Mitchell*
'incisors' (line 3): teeth at the front of the mouth

Questions to discuss
What effect has the poet attempted to create by laying the poem out like this?
Write the poem out as prose to help you reach a conclusion.
What effect has the poet created by the use of repetition in the poem?

What are the poet's views on his society? How effectively does he present them?

I'm Explaining A Few Things   *Pablo Neruda*
Neruda's 'native land' is Chile.
The historical background to this poem is the Spanish Civil War.
'metaphysics' (line 2): the discussion of abstract ideas

Questions to discuss
At the heart of this poem is a powerful contrast between the past and the present. What impression do you gain of the poet's past and what details create this impression?
Why is 'Everything' (line 24) given a line to itself?
What details in the following 14 lines suggest the richness of life in Spain before the war?
Consider, in the rest of the poem, the effect of the examples of repetition and the effect of the imagery. What is the effect of writing 'Treacherous generals: see my dead house, look at broken Spain' as four lines? How and why is the last line repeated?

What 'few things' is Neruda explaining? How effectively does he do so?

80

Listen To Me *Kishwar Naheed*

Questions to discuss
Who do you think is the narrator of this poem?

Write a poem in a similar style, about any subject.

Brief Thoughts On Exactness *Miroslav Holub*

Questions to discuss
This poem is based on a strong contrast. With what is the world of mankind contrasted?

In what ways does Holub suggest that the world of mankind is violent and ridiculous?

Write about the last four lines of this poem. How do they tie in with the rest of the poem? You might think about the images in the poem, the ideas expressed, the tone, the contrasts, the way the lines are arranged on the page.

Waiting For The Barbarians *C. P. Cavafy*

Questions to discuss
In what period of history is this poem set? How can you tell?

Examine the contrast between the speaker's world and the barbarians. How does the speaker's world feel about the barbarians and vice versa? What, especially, is suggested by the last two lines?

Epitaph On A Tyrant *W. H. Auden*

Questions to discuss
What effect does the phrase 'of a kind' have on the meaning of line 1?

What does line 2 suggest about the tyrant? What does line 4 suggest about him?

After reading the final line, is there a sinister air about the word 'burst' in line 5?

What effect has Auden created by describing the children in the final line as 'little'?

What impression do you gain of the tyrant? How is that impression created?

The Educators *D. M. Black*

Questions to discuss
What impression do you gain of the teachers in the first 15 lines?
How do they contrast with the dwarf in lines 15–23?
What has happened to the Palace at the end of the poem?
What does the image in the final two lines suggest about the teachers?

What are D. M. Black's feelings about educators? How well does he express them?

I Saw A Jolly Hunter *Charles Causley*

Questions to discuss
What effect does Causley achieve by repeatedly using the word 'jolly'?
What impression do we get of the hunter in stanzas 3 and 4?
What is the effect of the last line?

Is this poem any more than a piece designed to entertain? Does it have more serious intentions? If so, what are they and how does Causley achieve them?

Hawk Roosting *Ted Hughes*
'buoyancy' (line 6): ability to float in water or air
'sophistry' (line 15): false or illogical reasoning

Questions to discuss
1 Read the poem carefully to yourself before reading it aloud. How would you describe the tone of this poem? What effect is created by the fact that the hawk speaks mainly in short sentences?
2 Is anything suggested about the hawk by the fact that it sits in the 'top' of the wood (line 1)?
3. What seems to be its main concern or interest? Does it show any other concern or interest?
4 How does it feel about the world around it in stanza 2?
5 What are the hawk's feelings about itself in stanza 3, especially the last line?
6 How is this attitude developed in the first two lines of stanza 4?
7 How does the idea suggested by 'sophistry' in line 15 tie in with the 'falsifying dream' of line 2? What statement is the hawk making about itself?
8 What contrast is there in the fourth line of stanza 4? What does this contrast suggest about the hawk?
9 If 'no arguments' assert the hawk's right, what does it think *does* assert its right? How does this tie in with the idea expressed in stanza 2? What are the tone and attitude of the hawk in the last three lines?

Suggestions for writing
Write about this poem as a political statement: what is the hawk saying about itself and its relationship with the world? What impression of the hawk is created by the constant use of the first person 'I', and by the shortness of the statements?

Everything New Is Better Than Everything Old *Bertolt Brecht*

Questions to discuss
Is Brecht serious when he writes that 'Everything new is better than everything old' or is he being ironic?

Would you agree that 'A man who puts on a clean shirt/Is a new man'?
What point is Brecht making in the final section?

*What sort of world does Brecht describe in this poem? What does he feel
about it and how does he present his feelings?*

The Unknown Citizen   *W. H. Auden*

Title: several nations have honoured a representative dead soldier by building
a monument to him. To make the monument really representative they have
buried beneath it an unidentified dead soldier—a man whose name is
unknown.

'a scab' (line 9): someone who refuses to join a strike

'the Instalment Plan' (line 19): buying things on hire purchase

'Eugenist' (line 26): someone who believes that you can improve the quality
of the human race by selective breeding

Questions to discuss

This unknown citizen appears not to have had a name. What does his 'title'
('JS/07/M/378') suggest about the State's attitude towards its citizens?

Who has been asked about this citizen?

Does this suggest anything about the society that Auden is indirectly
describing?

What qualities do we think are saint-like? What qualities in the world of the
poem are saint-like? What does this suggest about the world that Auden is
describing?

What are the 'advantages of the Instalment Plan'? What are the disadvan-
tages?

What does the presence of a Eugenist, presumably in an official capacity,
suggest about the society?

What effect does line 24 have? What does it suggest about society's
expectations of its citizens?

What is the tone of the last two lines?

*In this poem, Auden is warning us against a certain type of society. Exactly
what is he warning us against and how effectively does he do so?*

Buy One Now   *D. J. Enright*

'(Pat. pend.)' (line 4): short for 'patent pending' which means that a
manufacturer has applied to the government to be granted the exclusive right
to produce a new product

Questions to discuss

To what does Enright compare the 'new sort of Poem'?

What is his attitude to the 'new sort of Poem'?

What does he think of people's attitude to life?

What does he think of poets' attitudes to poetry?

Common Sense *Alan Brownjohn*

Questions to discuss

What effect is Brownjohn trying to achieve by cutting up extracts from an arithmetic book in this way? Consider firstly the title and then the poem, stanza by stanza: what is the attitude of the writer of the arithmetic book to the people in the mathematical problems? Bearing in mind the first six stanzas, what does the final stanza suggest about ways to climb the educational ladder?

A Consumer's Report *Peter Porter*

Questions to discuss
What different things is life compared to in the poem?
What is the tone of the poem?
What do you think is the writer's attitude to life?
Does the poem affect the way you think about life and how it should be lived?

Cleator Moor *Norman Nicholson*

Write about this poem in any way that seems interesting to you. You may wish to consider two or more of the following topics:
—the theme or idea of the poem
—powerful use of language and imagery
—the form of the poem
—the use and effect of rhyme and half-rhyme.

Dulce Et Decorum Est *Wilfred Owen*

This poem was written during the First World War partly as a protest against the attitude to the war in England. The war had been thought to be glorious; men and boys were eager to fight and to gain glory.
'Dulce et decorum est/Pro patria mori' (lines 27–28): this sentence is taken from the Roman poet Horace, meaning 'It is sweet and honourable to die for one's country'

Questions to discuss
What do the similes in lines 1 and 2 suggest about the soldiers?
What does the word 'haunting' in line 3 add to the atmosphere?
What does the word 'trudge' in line 4 suggest about the soldiers?
What is the effect created by the repetition of 'all' in line 6?
What makes line 9 particularly dramatic?
Why are lines 15 and 16 separate from the rest of the poem?
What details in the final 14 lines effectively present the horror of the soldier's death?
Why is 'Lie' in the penultimate line given a capital letter?
What is the tone of the final two lines?

Is this poem an effective protest against the horrors of war? If so, what details make it effective?

Military Two-Step   *Cecil Rajendra*

'T.N.T.': trinitrotoluene, a type of powerful explosive
'two-step': a dance with long, sliding steps

Questions to discuss

This poem is satirical. 'Satire' can be defined as the ridicule of vice or folly. How does the satire work in this poem?

Try writing a satire of your own, about something you think is unjust or foolish.

Song Of The Banana Man   *Evan Jones*

'Golden Grove', 'Portland': places in Jamaica
'mullet and junga': fish
'Gros Michel', 'Lacatan': types of banana
'Massa': master
'John Crow': a scavenging bird
'Zekiel, Breda and Duppy Son': friends of the Banana man

Questions to discuss

How could you tell this is a song, if you didn't know the title?

Politics   *Sarah Goossens*

Questions to discuss

This poem is written as a ballad: what advantages and disadvantages does this have?

What does this poem have in common with a fable? Does it, for example, have a moral?

What is the tone of the poet? What stance does she adopt? Look especially at stanzas 5 and 7.

Write an assessment of this poem. You might like to comment on the effect of form, rhythm, and rhyme.

Section 4

Featured Poets

John Betjeman, Langston Hughes and Sylvia Plath

*J*OHN BETJEMAN was born in 1906 and died in 1985. He had a passion for English architecture and was noted for his knowledge and enthusiasm for the subject, making a series of television programmes during the 1970s.

His poetry is noted for its social commentary, its wit and its peculiar 'English' character. But far from being merely a writer of 'light' verse, Betjeman manages to combine a sometimes comic lightness with a serious message, couched in superbly written and traditionally arranged poetry.

*S*YLVIA PLATH grew up in the U.S.A. and met her husband, the poet Ted Hughes, while at Cambridge. They lived in London, Yorkshire and Devon, and had two children. She died in 1963, before much of her poetry was published.

The poems in this selection reflect various moods and situations, from the buoyant to the bleak, from having children to self-reflection. The poems, which are printed in chronological order, represent only a small part of her tremendous output from 1956 to 1963.

*L*ANGSTON HUGHES was born in Missouri, U.S.A. in 1902. He left high school and spent a year in Mexico before attending Columbia University for one year only. His first poem was published when he was nineteen and his first book of poetry when he was twenty-four. His poems caused him to be awarded a scholarship to Lincoln University in Pennsylvania and he graduated in 1929.

He won several prizes and gained various awards and fellowships during his life which he spent, from 1926 until his death in 1967, writing and lecturing. He wrote poetry, short stories, autobiography, song lyrics, essays and plays. His autobiography is entitled *The Big Sea* and is published by Pluto Press.

John
Betjeman

Executive

I am a young executive. No cuffs than mine are cleaner;
I have a Slimline brief-case and I use the firm's Cortina.
In every roadside hostelry from here to Burgess Hill
The *maîtres d'hôtel* all know me well and let me sign the bill.

You ask me what it is I do. Well actually, you know,
I'm partly a liaison man and partly P.R.O.
Essentially I integrate the current export drive
And basically I'm viable from ten o'clock till five.

For vital off-the-record work—that's talking transport wise—
I've a scarlet Aston-Martin—and does she go? She flies!   10
Pedestrians and dogs and cats—we mark them down for slaughter.
I also own a speed-boat which has never touched the water.

She's built of fibre-glass, of course. I call her 'Mandy Jane'
After a bird I used to know—No soda, please, just plain—
And how did I acquire her? Well to tell you about that
And to put you in the picture I must wear my other hat.

I do some mild developing. The sort of place I need
Is a quiet country market town that's rather run to seed.
A luncheon and a drink or two, a little *savoir faire*—
I fix the Planning Officer, the Town Clerk and the Mayor.   20

And if some preservationist attempts to interfere
A 'dangerous structure' notice from the Borough Engineer
Will settle any buildings that are standing in our way—
The modern style, sir, with respect, has really come to stay.

Hunter Trials

It's awf'lly bad luck on Diana,
  Her ponies have swallowed their bits;
She fished down their throats with a spanner
  And frightened them all into fits.

So now she's attempting to borrow.
  Do lend her some bits, Mummy, *do*;
I'll lend her my own for to-morrow,
  But to-day *I'*ll be wanting them too.

Just look at Prunella on Guzzle,
  The wizardest pony on earth;   *10*
Why doesn't she slacken his muzzle
  And tighten the breech in his girth?

I say, Mummy, there's Mrs. Geyser
  And doesn't she look pretty sick?
I bet it's because Mona Lisa
  Was hit on the hock with a brick.

Miss Blewitt says Monica threw it,
  But Monica says it was Joan,
And Joan's very thick with Miss Blewitt,
  So Monica's sulking alone.   *20*

And Margaret failed in her paces,
  Her withers got tied in a noose,
So her coronets caught in the traces
  And now all her fetlocks are loose.

Oh, it's me now. I'm terribly nervous.
  I wonder if Smudges will shy.
She's practically certain to swerve as
  Her Pelham is over one eye.

            *   *   *

Oh wasn't it naughty of Smudges?
  Oh, Mummy, I'm sick with disgust.   *30*
She threw me in front of the Judges,
  And my silly old collarbone's bust.

Pot Pourri From A Surrey Garden

Miles of pram in the wind and Pam in the gorse track,
  Coco-nut smell of the broom, and a packet of Weights
Press'd in the sand. The thud of a hoof on a horse-track—
    A horse-riding horse for a horse-track—
    Conifer county of Surrey approached
  Through remarkable wrought-iron gates.

Over your boundary now, I wash my face in a bird-bath,
  Then which path shall I take? that over there by the pram?
Down by the pond! or—yes, I will take the slippery third path,
    Trodden away with gym shoes,   *10*
    Beautiful fir-dry alley that leads
  To the bountiful body of Pam.

Pam, I adore you, Pam, you great big mountainous sports girl,
  Whizzing them over the net, full of the strength of five:
That old Malvernian brother, you zephyr and khaki shorts girl,
    Although he's playing for Woking,
    Can't stand up
  To your wonderful backhand drive.

See the strength of her arm, as firm and hairy as Hendren's;
  See the size of her thighs, the pout of her lips as, cross,   *20*
And full of a pent-up strength, she swipes at the rhododendrons,
    Lucky the rhododendrons,
    And flings her arrogant love-lock
  Back with a petulant toss.

Over the redolent pinewoods, in at the bathroom casement,
  One fine Saturday, Windlesham bells shall call:
Up the Butterfield aisle rich with Gothic enlacement,
    Licensed now for embracement,
    Pam and I, as the organ
  Thunders over you all.   *30*

Death In Leamington

She died in the upstairs bedroom
   By the light of the ev'ning star
That shone through the plate glass window
   From over Leamington Spa.

Beside her the lonely crochet
   Lay patiently and unstirred,
But the fingers that would have work'd it
   Were dead as the spoken word.

And Nurse came in with the tea-things
   Breast high 'mid the stands and chairs—
But Nurse was alone with her own little soul,
   And the things were alone with theirs.

She bolted the big round window,
   She let the blinds unroll,
She set a match to the mantle,
   She covered the fire with coal.

And "Tea!" she said in a tiny voice
   "Wake up! It's nearly *five*."
Oh! Chintzy, chintzy cheeriness,
   Half dead and half alive!

Do you know that the stucco is peeling?
   Do you know that the heart will stop?
From those yellow Italianate arches
   Do you hear the plaster drop?

Nurse looked at the silent bedstead,
   At the grey, decaying face,
As the calm of a Leamington ev'ning
   Drifted into the place.

She moved the table of bottles
   Away from the bed to the wall;
And tiptoeing gently over the stairs
   Turned down the gas in the hall.

Indoor Games Near Newbury

In among the silver birches winding ways of tarmac wander
  And the signs to Bussock Bottom, Tussock Wood and Windy Brake,
Gabled lodges, tile-hung churches, catch the lights of our Lagonda
  As we drive to Wendy's party, lemon curd and Christmas cake.

      Rich the makes of motor whirring,
      Past the pine-plantation purring
          Come up, Hupmobile, Delage!
      Short the way your chauffeurs travel,
      Crunching over private gravel
          Each from out his warm garáge.   10

Oh but Wendy, when the carpet yielded to my indoor pumps
      There you stood, your gold hair streaming,
      Handsome in the hall-light gleaming
There you looked and there you led me off into the game of clumps
      Then the new Victrola playing
      And your funny uncle saying
'Choose your partners for a fox-trot! Dance until it's *tea* o'clock!'
  'Come on, young 'uns, foot it featly!'
  Was it chance that paired us neatly,
  I, who loved you so completely,   20
You, who pressed me closely to you, hard against your party frock?

'Meet me when you've finished eating!' So we met and no one found
             us.
  Oh that dark and furry cupboard while the rest played hide and
             seek!
Holding hands our two hearts beating in the bedroom silence round
             us,
  Holding hands and hardly hearing sudden footstep, thud and shriek.
      Love that lay too deep for kissing—
      'Where *is* Wendy? Wendy's missing!'
          Love so pure it *had* to end,
      Love so strong that I was frighten'd
      When you gripped my fingers tight and   30
Hugging, whispered 'I'm your friend.'

Good-bye Wendy! Send the fairies, pinewood elf and larch tree gnome,
  Spingle-spangled stars are peeping
  At the lush Lagonda creeping
Down the winding ways of tarmac to the leaded lights of home.
  There, among the silver birches,
  All the bells of all the churches
Sounded in the bath-waste running out into the frosty air.
  Wendy speeded my undressing,
  Wendy is the sheet's caressing   40
  Wendy bending gives a blessing,
Holds me as I drift to dreamland, safe inside my slumberwear.

Senex

Oh would I could subdue the flesh
    Which sadly troubles me!
And then perhaps could view the flesh
As though I never knew the flesh
    And merry misery.

To see the golden hiking girl
    With wind about her hair,
The tennis-playing, biking girl,
The wholly-to-my-liking girl,
    To see and not to care.   *10*

At sundown on my tricycle
    I tour the Borough's edge,
And icy as an icicle
See bicycle by bicycle
    Stacked waiting in the hedge.

Get down from me! I thunder there,
    You spaniels! Shut your jaws!
Your teeth are stuffed with underwear,
Suspenders torn asunder there
    And buttocks in your paws!   *20*

Oh whip the dogs away my Lord,
    They make me ill with lust.
Bend bare knees down to pray, my Lord,
Teach sulky lips to say, my Lord,
    That flaxen hair is dust.

Notes and activities

You might like to consider the following ways of working on these poems:

1   Two of the poems in this selection have death as a theme. First identify the poems, and then write an essay comparing the two and saying, at the end, which one you prefer and why.
2   The other poems are less serious in theme as well as in tone. But what else do they have in common? Which poem is least like the others? Why?
3   Many of Betjeman's poems have to be read aloud to be appreciated fully. With a tape-recorder or for live performance, prepare a reading of two or three poems in groups of two or three.
4   If you prefer Betjeman to the other featured authors in this section, try writing an essay to explain your preference.

Further Reading

Betjeman's *Collected Poems* is published by John Murray, but Penguin publish a volume called *The Best of Betjeman*. You can also obtain recordings of his own readings of his work: *Betjeman's Banana Blush*.

Executive

'Cortina': the Ford Cortina, a car current in the '60s and favoured by travelling businessmen
'maîtres d'hôtel': head waiters or landlords
'P.R.O.': Public Relations Officer
'Aston-Martin': a sports car
'savoir faire': knowing how to do it

Hunter Trials

Title: 'hunter trials' are test outings for horses
'very thick with': very 'in' with
'withers': the ridge between the shoulder-bones of a horse
'coronets': the part of a horse's foot just above the hoof
'traces': straps
'fetlocks': just above the coronets
'shy': in the sense of shying away from a fence
'Pelham': a type of bit

Pot Pourri From A Surrey Garden

Title: a 'pot pourri' (pronounced 'po pouree') is a mixture of dried petals, kept in a bowl to give a pleasant smell to a room

'Weights': a brand of cigarette

'Malvernian': Malvern, an English boys' boarding school

'redolent': smelling suggestively of

'Butterfield': a Victorian architect

Death In Leamington

'Leamington': a suburb in the Midlands

'mantle': part of a gas light

'chintzy': cheap and gaudy

'stucco': plaster

Indoor Games Near Newbury

'Lagonda': a very expensive car

'clumps': a parlour game of question and answer

'Victrola': an early record-player

'foot it featly': a silly way of saying 'dance it well'

Sylvia
Plath

Southern Sunrise

Color of lemon, mango, peach,
These storybook villas
Still dream behind
Shutters, their balconies
Fine as hand-
Made lace, or a leaf-and-flower pen-sketch.

Tilting with the winds,
On arrowy stems,
Pineapple-barked,
A green crescent of palms   *10*
Sends up its forked
Firework of fronds.

A quartz-clear dawn
Inch by bright inch
Gilds all our Avenue,
And out of the blue drench
Of Angels' Bay
Rises the round red watermelon sun.

Fiesta Melons

In Benidorm there are melons,
Whole donkey-carts full

Of innumerable melons,
Ovals and balls,

Bright green and thumpable
Laced over with stripes

Of turtle-dark green.
Choose an egg-shape, a world-shape,

Bowl one homeward to taste
In the whitehot noon: *10*

Cream-smooth honeydews,
Pink-pulped whoppers,

Bump-rinded cantaloupes
With orange cores.

Each wedge wears a studding
Of blanched seeds or black seeds

To strew like confetti
Under the feet of

This market of melon-eating
Fiesta-goers.   *20*

Morning Song

Love set you going like a fat gold watch.
The midwife slapped your footsoles, and your bald cry
Took its place among the elements.

Our voices echo, magnifying your arrival. New statue.
In a drafty museum, your nakedness
Shadows our safety. We stand round blankly as walls.

I'm no more your mother
Than the cloud that distils a mirror to reflect its own slow
Effacement at the wind's hand.

All night your moth-breath   *10*
Flickers among the flat pink roses. I wake to listen:
A far sea moves in my ear.

One cry, and I stumble from bed, cow-heavy and floral
In my Victorian nightgown.
Your mouth opens clean as a cat's. The window square

Whitens and swallows its dull stars. And now you try
Your handful of notes;
The clear vowels rise like balloons.

Mushrooms

Overnight, very
Whitely, discreetly,
Very quietly

Our toes, our noses
Take hold on the loam,
Acquire the air.

Nobody sees us,
Stops us, betrays us;
The small grains make room.

Soft fists insist on   10
Heaving the needles,
The leafy bedding,

Even the paving.
Our hammers, our rams,
Earless and eyeless,

Perfectly voiceless,
Widen the crannies,
Shoulder through holes. We

Diet on water,
On crumbs of shadow,   20
Bland-mannered, asking

Little or nothing.
So many of us!
So many of us!

We are shelves, we are
Tables, we are meek,
We are edible,

Nudgers and shovers
In spite of ourselves.
Our kind multiplies: 30

We shall by morning
Inherit the earth.
Our foot's in the door.

You're

Clownlike, happiest on your hands,
Feet to the stars, and moon-skulled,
Gilled like a fish. A common-sense
Thumbs-down on the dodo's mode.
Wrapped up in yourself like a spool,
Trawling your dark as owls do.
Mute as a turnip from the Fourth
Of July to All Fools' Day,
O high-riser, my little loaf.

Vague as fog and looked for like mail.　　　　　　　　　10
Farther off than Australia.
Bent-backed Atlas, our travelled prawn.
Snug as a bud and at home
Like a sprat in a pickle jug.
A creel of eels, all ripples.
Jumpy as a Mexican bean.
Right, like a well-done sum.
A clean slate, with your own face on.

Blackberrying

Nobody in the lane, and nothing, nothing but blackberries,
Blackberries on either side, though on the right mainly,
A blackberry alley, going down in hooks, and a sea
Somewhere at the end of it, heaving. Blackberries
Big as the ball of my thumb, and dumb as eyes
Ebon in the hedges, fat
With blue-red juices. These they squander on my fingers.
I had not asked for such a blood sisterhood; they must love me.
They accommodate themselves to my milkbottle, flattening their
  sides.

Overhead go the choughs in black, cacophonous flocks—   *10*
Bits of burnt paper wheeling in a blown sky.
Theirs is the only voice, protesting, protesting.
I do not think the sea will appear at all.
The high, green meadows are glowing, as if lit from within.
I come to one bush of berries so ripe it is a bush of flies,
Hanging their bluegreen bellies and their wing panes in a Chinese
  screen.
The honey-feast of the berries has stunned them; they believe in
  heaven.
One more hook, and the berries and bushes end.

The only thing to come now is the sea.
From between two hills a sudden wind funnels at me,   *20*
Slapping its phantom laundry in my face.
These hills are too green and sweet to have tasted salt.
I follow the sheep path between them. A last hook brings me
To the hills' northern face, and the face is orange rock
That looks out on nothing, nothing but a great space
Of white and pewter lights, and a din like silversmiths
Beating and beating at an intractable metal.

Mirror

I am silver and exact. I have no preconceptions.
Whatever I see I swallow immediately
Just as it is, unmisted by love or dislike.
I am not cruel, only truthful—
The eye of a little god, four-cornered.
Most of the time I meditate on the opposite wall.
It is pink, with speckles. I have looked at it so long
I think it is a part of my heart. But it flickers.
Faces and darkness separate us over and over.

Now I am a lake. A woman bends over me,   *10*
Searching my reaches for what she really is.
Then she turns to those liars, the candles or the moon.
I see her back, and reflect it faithfully.
She rewards me with tears and an agitation of hands.
I am important to her. She comes and goes.
Each morning it is her face that replaces the darkness.
In me she has drowned a young girl, and in me an old woman
Rises toward her day after day, like a terrible fish.

Notes and activities

You might like to consider the following ways of working on these poems:

For reading and discussion
1   Read and complete the written work on 'Mirror' and discuss.
2   Read the rest of the poems for homework.
3   Then discuss the following statements in small groups:
    —all of these are depressing poems
    —the best poem is 'Mushrooms'
    —the most difficult one is 'Mirror'.
4   Report to the class and discuss these points with the class as a whole.

For coursework folders

1   Group the poems in terms of what they have in common (you might find various ways of grouping them). Then write about the group of poems that appeals to you most, comparing it to one other group and saying why you prefer the poems in your chosen group.
2   The poems are arranged in chronological order. Can you trace any development from 'Southern Sunrise' to 'Mirror'?
3   If you had to choose just one poem to represent Sylvia Plath as a writer, which one would it be? Use this one as the focus of your essay, referring to others in the course of your piece.

Further reading

If you want to read more of Sylvia Plath's work—or even write a longer piece on her writing—look for the following books:
>   *Collected Poems* (1981)
>   *The Colossus* (1960)
>   *Ariel* (1965)
>   *Crossing the Water* (1971)
>   *Winter Trees* (1971)

She has written a novel, *The Bell Jar* (1963), and a collection of her stories and occasional pieces was published under the title *Johnny Panic and the Bible of Dreams* in 1977. There is also a collection of her letters to her mother, *Letters Home* (1975).

Southern Sunrise

The 'South' of the title is probably both that of the southern states of the U.S.A. and of Spain, where Plath lived in the summer of 1956. It is a generalised 'South', suggesting richness and heat to those from the colder, less exotic North of England or Boston.

Fiesta Melons

'fiesta': holiday, festival
'Benidorm': now a built-up holiday resort on the coast of Spain, but in 1956 an undeveloped fishing village

Morning Song

Dated 19th February 1961, when her baby was ten months old

Mushrooms

Plath writes, 'Wrote an exercise on Mushrooms yesterday which Ted (Hughes) likes. And I do too. My absolute lack of judgement when I've written something: whether it's trash or genius.' (*Collected Poems* p 289)
'inherit the earth': this plays on the Biblical line 'The meek shall inherit the earth'

You're

Sylvia Plath and Ted Hughes had a baby girl, Frieda, on 1st April 1960, but the poem is dated 'January/February 1960'.

Blackberrying

Probably written in Devon or Cornwall 'in a cliff cove looking out on to the Atlantic'
'ebon': ebony, black
'choughs': jackdaws
'intractable': stubborn

Questions to discuss
See 'Blackberry-Picking' and 'In that year, 1914 ...' in the *Poems for Comparison* section. You might like to compare either or both of those poems with this one.

Mirror

This is a difficult poem in two nine line stanzas. As with many poems, the title is important. It gives us a powerful clue as to who the poem's speaker is.

Questions for writing

1. What is the mirror's attitude to itself? Note particularly lines 1, 3, 4 and 13.
2. What is suggested about the mirror by the adjective 'silver' in line 1?
3. What idea in line 2 is taken up again by the image of the lake and particularly by the simile in line 18?
4. How is 'Just as it is' (line 3) given greater emphasis? Why is this idea important? With what ideas in lines 1 and 4 does it link?
5. How does the adjective 'unmisted' in line 3 tie in with the poem as a whole?
6. What do 'love' and 'dislike' have in common and how might they 'mist' the way we see things?
7. What is suggested by the mirror referring to itself (line 5) as a 'little god'?
8. What quality does the wall have which makes it seem natural for the mirror to regard itself as 'a part of my heart'?
9. Why did Plath link 'faces' and 'darkness' in line 9?
10. What makes the opening of the second stanza dramatic?
11. What does the word 'liars' (line 12) suggest about the mirror?
12. What is the mirror's attitude to the woman? Note line 13.
13. What is the woman's attitude to the mirror and what is her reaction to what she sees? Why?
14. What is the connection between lines 15/16 and line 9?
15. What two images in the last two lines are particularly disturbing? Do they contrast with what has gone before them? What effect does this have on the reader?
16. What does 'Day after day' suggest about the woman and about ageing?
17. Does the mirror's attitude to itself (see question 1) change in the poem or does it help to unify the poem? What else do you think gives the poem unity?

Keeping in mind your ideas in response to these questions, attempt to assess the poem as a whole. The following questions may also suggest an approach:

Is 'Mirror' merely a whimsical poem about a mirror? Does it suggest ideas about human vanity? Does it communicate feelings about ageing and security? Does it suggest anything about human beings or human relationships?

Langston
Hughes

Mama And Daughter

Mama, please brush off my coat.
I'm going down the street.

Where're you going, daughter?

To see my sugar-sweet.

Who is your sugar, honey?
Turn around—I'll brush behind.

He is that young man, mama,
I can't get off my mind.

Daughter, once upon a time—
Let me brush the hem—   10
Your father, yes, he was the one!
I felt like that about him.

But it was a long time ago
He up and went his way.
I hope that wild young son-of-a-gun
Rots in hell today!

Mama, dad couldn't be still young.

He *was* young yesterday.
He *was* young when he—
Turn around!
So I can brush your back, I say!

Delinquent

Little Julie
Has grown quite tall.
Folks say she don't like
To stay home at all.

Little Julie
Has grown quite stout.
Folks say it's not just
Stomach sticking out.

Little Julie
Has grown quite wise—   10
A tiger, a lion, and an owl
In her eyes.

Little Julie
Says she don't care!
What she means is:
Nobody cares
Anywhere.

S-sss-ss-sh!

Her great adventure ended
As great adventures should
In life being created
Anew—and good.

> *Except the neighbors*
> *And her mother*
> *Did not think it good!*

Nature has a way
Of not caring much
About marriage   *10*
Licenses and such.

> *But the neighbors*
> *And her mother*
> *Cared very much!*

The baby came one morning,
Almost with the sun.

> *The neighbors—*
> *And its grandma—*
> *Were outdone!*

But mother and child   *20*
Thought it fun.

Hard Daddy

I went to ma daddy,
Says Daddy I have got the blues.
Went to ma daddy,
Says Daddy I have got the blues.
Ma daddy says, Honey,
Can't you bring no better news?

I cried on his shoulder but
He turned his back on me.
Cried on his shoulder but
He turned his back on me.   *10*
He said a woman's cryin's
Never gonna bother me.

I wish I had wings to
Fly like the eagle flies.
Wish I had wings to
Fly like the eagle flies.
I'd fly on ma man an'
I'd scratch out both his eyes.

Little Old Letter

It was yesterday morning
I looked in my box for mail.
The letter that I found there
Made me turn right pale.

Just a little old letter,
Wasn't even one page long—
But it made me wish
I was in my grave and gone.

I turned it over,
Not a word writ on the back.   *10*
I never felt so lonesome
Since I was born black.

Just a pencil and paper,
You don't need no gun nor knife—
A little old letter
Can take a person's life.

Ruby Brown

She was young and beautiful
And golden like the sunshine
That warmed her body.
And because she was colored
Mayville had no place to offer her,
Nor fuel for the clean flame of joy
That tried to burn within her soul.

One day,
Sitting on old Mrs. Latham's back porch
Polishing the silver,   *10*
She asked herself two questions
And they ran something like this:
What can a colored girl do
On the money from a white woman's kitchen?
And ain't there any joy in this town?

Now the streets down by the river
Know more about this pretty Ruby Brown,
And the sinister shuttered houses of the bottoms
Hold a yellow girl
Seeking an answer to her questions.   *20*
The good church folk do not mention
Her name any more.

But the white men,
Habitués of the high shuttered houses,
Pay more money to her now
Than they ever did before,
When she worked in their kitchens.

Puzzled

Here on the edge of hell
Stands Harlem—
Remembering the old lies,
The old kicks in the back,
The old, *Be patient*,
They told us before.

Sure, we remember.
Now, when the man at the corner store
Says sugar's gone up another two cents,
And bread one, 10
And there's a new tax on cigarettes—
We remember the job we never had,
Never could get,
And can't have now
Because we're colored.

So we stand here
On the edge of hell
In Harlem
And look out on the world
And wonder 20
What we're gonna do
In the face of
What we remember.

Ballad Of The Landlord

Landlord, landlord,
My roof has sprung a leak.
Don't you 'member I told you about it
Way last week?

Landlord, landlord,
These steps is broken down.
When you come up yourself
It's a wonder you don't fall down.

Ten Bucks you say I owe you?
Ten Bucks you say is due?   *10*
Well, that's Ten Bucks more'n I'll pay you
Till you fix this house up new.

What? You gonna get eviction orders?
You gonna cut off my heat?
You gonna take my furniture and
Throw it in the street?

Um-huh! You talking high and mighty.
Talk on—till you get through.
You ain't gonna be able to say a word
If I land my fist on you.   *20*

Police! Police!
Come and get this man!
He's trying to ruin the government
And overturn the land!

Copper's whistle!
Patrol bell!
Arrest.

Precinct Station.
Iron cell.
Headlines in press:

MAN THREATENS LANDLORD

TENANT HELD NO BAIL

JUDGE GIVES NEGRO 90 DAYS IN COUNTY JAIL

Notes and activities

You may like to consider some of the following questions:

1 Several of these poems are concerned with human relationships. What is the nature of the relationships in 'Mama And Daughter' and 'Hard Daddy' and what feelings are revealed?

2 Read 'Delinquent' and 'S-sss-ss-sh!' What is the situation of each of these two poems? What is Hughes's attitude to their situation?

3 Both 'Little Old Letter' and 'Hard Daddy' are very like song lyrics. What similarities and what differences can you see between these poems and song lyrics? How effectively are the speakers' feelings communicated in these two poems?

4 'Ballad Of The Landlord', 'Ruby Brown' and 'Delinquent' all tell stories with morals. What are the stories and what are the morals? What do you think these poems gain or lose by being written as poems?

5 How would you read 'Puzzled', 'S-sss-ss-sh!' and 'Little Old Letter' aloud? What is the tone of these three poems? How can you tell? Is the tone in each of them the same throughout? Where, if at all, does the tone change and what does the change tell us about the mood of the speaker?

Section 5

Poems for Comparison

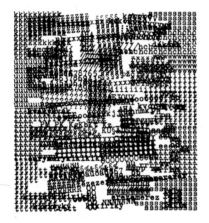

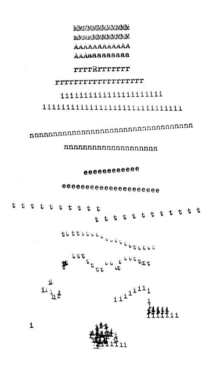

SCHWITTERS, Evident poem

MARINETTI, Evident poem

Jiří Kolář

*T*his section is intended to enable you to practise writing about unseen poetry and we have provided a minimum of notes. We have suggested that you compare the poems that follow; of course, you can write about the poems separately but it is often easier to see a poem more clearly when you have something with which to compare it.

You may wish to take a sheet of paper, when comparing poems, and on one side write down similarities and on the other side differences; you might wish to use subheadings on your sheet. You could be looking to compare subject matter, situation, theme, language, form, rhythm, rhyme and tone. For example, with 'Vergissmeinnicht' and 'Sleeper In A Valley' there is a similarity of subject matter: both poems describe a dead soldier but what the poets see in the dead soldiers—the feelings that the dead soldiers arouse—is very different; with 'What The Chairman Told Tom' and 'To The Public' the common theme has to do with the nature of poetry and poets; their tones are not dissimilar but the language is very different in terms of register and the forms differ greatly; in 'Picture Of A Girl' and 'Neutral Tones' the situations are similar as both poets reflect on a past relationship but their tones are far from similar; the extract from 'The Destruction Of Sennacherib' and 'Very Like A Whale' take us into the realm of parody: what is Nash suggesting about simile and metaphor? Does what he says make you view Byron's poem differently? Compare their use of line length: why does Nash vary his so much? All the time you should be concentrating on the effects that the poets achieve. Never be content simply to say what they have done ('the poet has written in four line stanzas', say) but try to see why they have done it and what effect it has ('the four line rhymed stanzas give the poem an impression of simplicity, of the ballad', say).

We feel that it is probably best, after making notes about both poems, that you write about the poems separately; finish writing about one before you begin writing about the other; but try to stress similarities and contrasts. We hope that you will find it illuminating to compare poems in this way and that it will enable you not to enjoy one poem at the expense of another but to perceive the strengths and techniques of both.

What The Chairman Told Tom

Poetry? It's a hobby.
I run model trains.
Mr Shaw there breeds pigeons.

It's not work. You don't sweat.
Nobody pays for it.
You *could* advertise soap.

Arts, that's opera; or repertory—
The Desert Song.
Nancy was in the chorus.

But to ask for twelve pounds a week—   *10*
married, aren't you?—
you've got a nerve.

How could I look a bus conductor
in the face
if I paid you twelve pounds?

Who says it's poetry, anyhow?
My ten year old
can do it *and* rhyme.

I get three thousand and expenses,
a car, vouchers,   *20*
but I'm an accountant.

They do what I tell them,
my company.
What do *you* do?

Nasty little words, nasty long words,
it's unhealthy.
I want to wash when I meet a poet.

They're Reds, addicts,
all delinquents.
What you write is rot.   *30*

Mr Hines says so, and he's a schoolteacher,
he ought to know.
Go and find *work*.

Basil Bunting

To The Public

Why hold that poets are so sensitive?
A thickskinned grasping lot who filch and eavesdrop,
Who enjoy ourselves at other men's expense,
Who, legislators or not, ourselves are lawless,
We do not need your indulgence, much less your pity;
With fewer qualms, we have rather more common sense
Than your Common Man, also of course more freedom,
With our burglars' and gunmen's fingers, our green fingers.
So, crude though we are, we get to times and places
And, saving your presence or absence, will continue   10
Throwing our dreams and guts in people's faces.

Louis MacNeice

Picture Of A Girl

I lie on the dirty white candlewick
You so disliked, thinking of you at your best;
Among animals mostly—Absalom
Whose high, unearthly screech you mimicked once
So fluently, he swooped from his chimney perch
To strut before us on the rain-fresh lawn,
Rustling green plumage as if a mate
Had bloomed there like the cèpes and chanterelles ...
And then the cats; Babette, whose dynasty
Had frayed the Morris hangings into shreds—   10
I remember you struggling to hold all twelve
Still in your lap for a photograph;
That night you giggled quietly in your sleep—
Lovely transparent dreamer, I could see
The singed-beige kittens tumbling there again ...

Now I recede, the years are like rough stones
Glazed to a moonstone glimmer by the sea,
Fantastical—Absalom cries again,
I hear that garden crackling in the rain,
Pale dusty green mimosa's saffron burrs   20
Turning to paste as they brush our clothes,
Quicksilver raindrops on the soft peach furze—
We lived well, I remember starched linen,
Silver, the flayed blue hearts of hot-house figs,
My profligate goddess stooping where a marrow
Had burst with rain, and spilt its sequin seeds,
The clouds pitted like granite, but tissue-light,
Heaving their slow collisions in the skies,
And where the pond froze up one winter night
Big golden carp alive beneath the ice ...   30

James Lasdun

Neutral Tones

We stood by a pond that winter day,
And the sun was white, as though chidden of God,
And a few leaves lay on the starving sod;
    —They had fallen from an ash, and were gray.

Your eyes on me were as eyes that rove
Over tedious riddles of years ago;
And some words played between us to and fro
    On which lost the more by our love.

The smile on your mouth was the deadest thing
Alive enough to have strength to die;   *10*
And a grin of bitterness swept thereby
    Like an ominous bird a-wing. . . .

Since then, keen lessons that love deceives,
And wrings with wrong, have shaped to me
Your face, and the God-curst sun, and a tree,
    And a pond edged with grayish leaves.

Thomas Hardy

Winter Is Here

Winter is here again—

If I were young
perhaps I would sing
about the black bowl of earth
filled with the coolness of snowflowers,
perhaps the dew of the stars
would sparkle on the night-blue meadow of my song.

But the songs of my youth are frozen.
My song is poor and tired
like a woman   *10*
with knotty blue hands
gathering sticks
for the fire of her rickety cabin.

I am circling the track of my scanty bread,
cold like the courtyard of a prison.
My senses, my thoughts are rough with work.

Winter is here,
to sharpen misery,
to torture the children of need with the whip of his winds.
But the berries of the rowan-tree   *20*
are burning like beacon fires.

Katri Vala
Translated from Finnish by Jaakko A. Ahokas

Winter Night

A snowstorm made the earth tremble
through its whole frame.
A candle-flame upon a table,
only a candle-flame.

Like midges swarming in the summer,
winging to a spark,
the flakes flew in a thick shimmer
to the window from the dark.

The blizzard blew. Its rime and stubble
clung to the pane.   *10*
A candle-flame upon a table,
only a candle-flame.

High up on the bright-lit ceiling
shadows were tossed:
hands cross-clasped, feet cross-leaning,
fate in a cross.

And two small shoes fell with a clatter
to the floor, useless,
and wax drops from the night-light spattered
weeping upon a dress.   *20*

And all things faded, misted, feeble,
a grey-white dream.
A candle-flame upon a table,
only a candle-flame.

The candle felt a hidden shaking
blow hot temptation:
wings raised, like an angel's, taking
a cross-like station.

All February, storm rocked the gable
and found there the same   *30*
candle-flame upon a table,
only a candle-flame.

Boris Pasternak
Translated by Edwin Morgan

Humming Bird

The humming bird refuels
in mid-air from the hub
of a fuchsia flower.
Its belly is feathered white
as rapids; its eye
is smaller than a drop of tar.
A bodied moth, it beats
stopwatches into lethargy
with its wingstrokes.

Food it needs every fifteen   *10*
minutes. It has the metabolism
of a steam engine.
Its tiny claws are slight
as pared fingernail;
you could slip it with ease
into a breast pocket.
There it might lie, cowed
—or give you a second heart.

Paul Groves

Humming-Bird

I can imagine, in some otherworld
Primeval-dumb, far back
In that most awful stillness, that only gasped and hummed,
Humming-birds raced down the avenues.

Before anything had a soul,
While life was a heave of Matter, half inanimate,
This little bit chipped off in brilliance
And went whizzing through the slow, vast, succulent stems.

I believe there were no flowers then,
In the world where the humming-bird flashed ahead of creation.   *10*
I believe he pierced the slow vegetable veins with his long beak.

Probably he was big
As mosses, and little lizards, they say, were once big.
Probably he was a jabbing, terrifying monster.

We look at him through the wrong end of the long telescope of
  Time,
Luckily for us.

D. H. Lawrence

Blackberry-Picking

For Philip Hobsbaum

Late August, given heavy rain and .sun
For a full week, the blackberries would ripen.
At first, just one, a glossy purple clot
Among others, red, green, hard as a knot.
You ate that first one and its flesh was sweet
Like thickened wine: summer's blood was in it
Leaving stains upon the tongue and lust for
Picking. Then red ones inked up and that hunger
Sent us out with milk-cans, pea-tins, jam-pots
Where briars scratched and wet grass bleached our boots.   *10*
Round hayfields, cornfields and potato-drills
We trekked and picked until the cans were full,
Until the tinkling bottom had been covered
With green ones, and on top big dark blobs burned
Like a plate of eyes. Our hands were peppered
With thorn pricks, our palms sticky as Bluebeard's.

We hoarded the fresh berries in the byre.
But when the bath was filled we found a fur,
A rat-grey fungus, glutting on our cache.
The juice was stinking too. Once off the bush   *20*
The fruit fermented, the sweet flesh would turn sour.
I always felt like crying. It wasn't fair
That all the lovely canfuls smelt of rot.
Each year I hoped they'd keep, knew they would not.

Seamus Heaney

'In that year, 1914 ...'

'In that year, 1914, we lived on the farm
And the relatives lived with us.
A banner year for wild blackberries
Dad was crazy about wild blackberries
No berries like that now.
You know Kitsap County was logged before
The turn of the century—it was easiest of all,
Close to water, virgin timber,
When I was a kid walking about in the
Stumpland, wherever you'd go a skidroad   10
Puncheon, all overgrown.
We went up one like that, fighting our way through
To its end near the top of a hill:
For some reason wild blackberries
Grew best there. We took off one morning
Right after milking: rode the horses
To a valley we'd been to once before
Hunting berries, and hitched the horses.
About a quarter mile up the old road
We found the full ripe of berrytime—   20
And with only two pails—so we
Went back home, got Mother and Ruth,
And filled lots of pails. Mother sent letters
To all the relatives in Seattle:
Effie, Aunt Lucy, Bill Moore,
Forrest, Edna, six or eight, they all came
Out to the farm, and we didn't take pails
Then: we took copper clothes-boilers,
Wash-tubs, buckets, and all went picking.
We were canning for three days.'   30

Gary Snyder

127

Vergissmeinnicht

Three weeks gone and the combatants gone,
returning over the nightmare ground
we found the place again, and found
the soldier sprawling in the sun.

The frowning barrel of his gun
overshadowing. As we came on
that day, he hit my tank with one
like the entry of a demon.

Look. Here in the gunpit spoil
the dishonoured picture of his girl   10
who has put: *Steffi. Vergissmeinnicht*
in a copybook gothic script.

We see him almost with content
abased, and seeming to have paid
and mocked at by his own equipment
that's hard and good when he's decayed.

But she would weep to see today
how on his skin the swart flies move;
the dust upon the paper eye
and the burst stomach like a cave.   20

For here the lover and the killer are mingled
who had one body and one heart.
And death who had the soldier singled
has done the lover mortal hurt.

Keith Douglas

Sleeper In A Valley

Couched in a hollow, where a humming stream
Hooks, absently, sun-fragments, silver-white,
And from the proud hill-top beam falls on beam
Laving the valley in a foam of light,

A soldier sleeps, lips parted, bare his head,
His young neck pillowed where blue cresses drown;
He sprawls under a cloud, his truckle-bed
A spread of grass where the gold sky drips down.

His feet drift among reeds. He sleeps alone,
Smiling the pale smile that sick children wear.   10
Earth, nurse him fiercely! He is cold as stone,
And stilled his senses to the flowering air.

Hand on his breast, awash in the sun's tide
Calmly he sleeps; two red holes in his side.

Arthur Rimbaud
Translated by Charles Causley

'Anger lay by me all night long'

Anger lay by me all night long,
    His breath was hot upon my brow,
He told me of my burning wrong,
    All night he talked and would not go.

He stood by me all through the day,
    Struck from my hand the book, the pen;
He said: 'Hear first what I've to say,
    And sing, if you've the heart to, then.'

And can I cast him from my couch?
    And can I lock him from my room?   *10*
Ah no, his honest words are such
    That he's my true-lord, and my doom.

Elizabeth Daryush

A Poison Tree

I was angry with my friend:
I told my wrath, my wrath did end.
I was angry with my foe:
I told it not, my wrath did grow.

And I watered it in fears,
Night & morning with my tears;
And I sunned it with smiles,
And with soft deceitful wiles.

And it grew both day and night,
Till it bore an apple bright.   *10*
And my foe beheld it shine,
And he knew that it was mine.

And into my garden stole,
When the night had veiled the pole:
In the morning glad I see
My foe outstretched beneath the tree.

William Blake

Revelation

I remember once being shown the black bull
when a child at the farm for eggs and milk.
They called him Bob—as though perhaps
you could reduce a monster
with the charm of a friendly name.
At the threshold of his outhouse, someone
held my hand and let me peer inside.
At first, only black
And the hot reek of him. Then he was immense,
his edges merging with the darkness, just   *10*
a big bulk and a roar to be really scared of,
a trampling, and a clanking tense with the chain's jerk.
His eyes swivelled in the great wedge of his tossed head.
He roared his rage. His nostrils gaped.

And in the yard outside,
oblivious hens picked their way about.
The faint and rather festive tinkling
behind the mellow stone and hasp was all they knew
of that Black Mass, straining at his chains.
I had always half-known he existed—   *20*
this antidote and Anti-Christ his anarchy
threatening the eggs, well rounded, self-contained—
and the placidity of milk.
I ran, my pigtails thumping on my back in fear,
past the big boys in the farm lane
who pulled the wings from butterflies and
blew up frogs with straws.
Past throned hedge and harried nest,
scared of the eggs shattering—
only my small and shaking hand on the jug's rim   *30*
in case the milk should spill.

Liz Lochhead

The Bull Moses

A hoist up and I could lean over
The upper edge of the high half-door,
My left foot ledged on the hinge, and look in at the byre's
Blaze of darkness: a sudden shut-eyed look
Backward into the head.
                        Blackness is depth
Beyond star. But the warm weight of his breathing,
The ammoniac reek of his litter, the hotly-tongued
Mash of his cud, steamed against me.
Then, slowly, as onto the mind's eye—   *10*
The brow like masonry, the deep-keeled neck:
Something come up there onto the brink of the gulf,
Hadn't heard of the world, too deep in itself to be called to,
Stood in sleep. He would swing his muzzle at a fly
But the square of sky where I hung, shouting, waving,
Was nothing to him; nothing of our light
Found any reflection in him.
                      Each dusk the farmer led him
Down to the pond to drink and smell the air,
And he took no pace but the farmer   *20*
Led him to take it, as if he knew nothing
Of the ages and continents of his fathers,
Shut, while he wombed, to a dark shed
And steps between his door and the duckpond;
The weight of the sun and the moon and the world hammered
To a ring of brass through his nostrils.
                      He would raise
His streaming muzzle and look out over the meadows,
But the grasses whispered nothing awake, the fetch
Of the distance drew nothing to momentum   *30*
In the locked black of his powers. He came strolling gently back,
Paused neither toward the pig-pens on his right,
Nor toward the cow-byres on his left: something
Deliberate in his leisure, some beheld future
Founding in his quiet.
                  I kept the door wide,
Closed it after him and pushed the bolt.

Ted Hughes

The Destruction Of Sennacherib

I

The Assyrian came down like the wolf on the fold,
And his cohorts were gleaming in purple and gold;
And the sheen of their spears was like stars on the sea,
When the blue wave rolls nightly on deep Galilee.

II

Like the leaves of the forest when Summer is green,
That host with their banners at sunset were seen:
Like the leaves of the forest when Autumn hath blown,
That host on the morrow lay wither'd and strown.

III

For the Angel of Death spread his wings on the blast,
And breathed in the face of the foe as he pass'd;   10
And the eyes of the sleepers wax'd deadly and chill,
And their hearts but once heaved, and for ever grew still!

Lord Byron

Very Like A Whale

One thing that literature would be greatly the better for
Would be a more restricted employment by authors of simile and
  metaphor.
Authors of all races, be they Greeks, Romans, Teutons or Celts,
Can't seem just to say that anything is the thing it is but have to go
  out of their way to say that it is like something else.

134

What does it mean when we are told

That the Assyrian came down like a wolf on the fold?

In the first place, George Gordon Byron had had enough
experience

To know that it probably wasn't just one Assyrian, it was a lot of
Assyrians.

However, as too many arguments are apt to induce apoplexy and
thus hinder longevity,

We'll let it pass as one Assyrian for the sake of brevity.   10

Now then, this particular Assyrian, the one whose cohorts were
gleaming in purple and gold,

Just what does the poet mean when he says he came down like a
wolf on the fold?

In heaven and earth more than is dreamed of in our philosophy
there are a great many things,

But I don't imagine that among them there is a wolf with purple
and gold cohorts or purple and gold anythings.

No, no, Lord Byron, before I'll believe that this Assyrian was actually
like a wolf I must have some kind of proof;

Did he run on all fours and did he have a hairy tail and a big red
mouth and big white teeth and did he say Woof woof woof?

Frankly I think it very unlikely, and all you were entitled to say, at
the very most,

Was that the Assyrian cohorts came down like a lot of Assyrian
cohorts about to destroy the Hebrew host.

But that wasn't fancy enough for Lord Byron, oh dear me no, he
had to invent a lot of figures of speech and then interpolate them.

With the result that whenever you mention Old Testament soldiers
to people they say Oh yes, they're the ones that a lot of wolves
dressed up in gold and purple ate them.   20

That's the kind of thing that's being done all the time by poets, from
Homer to Tennyson;

They're always comparing ladies to lilies and veal to venison,

And they always say things like that the snow is a white blanket after
a winter storm.

Oh it is, is it, all right then, you sleep under a six-inch blanket of
snow and I'll sleep under a half-inch blanket of unpoetical blanket
material and we'll see which one keeps warm,

And after that maybe you'll begin to comprehend dimly

What I mean by too much metaphor and simile.

Ogden Nash

Notes

What The Chairman Told Tom   *Basil Bunting*
'vouchers' (line 20): luncheon vouchers, which certain restaurants and cafés will accept instead of cash
'Reds' (line 28): Communists

with

To The Public   *Louis MacNeice*
'filch' (line 2): steal
'qualms' (line 6): uneasiness of conscience

Picture Of A Girl   *James Lasdun*
'candlewick' (line 1): a cotton material, usually used for bedspreads
'cèpes' (line 8): a French mushroom
'chanterelles' (line 8): an edible fungus
'profligate' (line 25): very extravagant

with

Neutral Tones   *Thomas Hardy*
'chidden' (line 2): scolded, rebuked
'sod' (line 3): earth

Winter Is Here   *Katri Vala (translated by Jaakko A. Ahokas)*
'rowan-tree' (line 19): a tree which has small, red berries

with

Winter Night   *Boris Pasternak (translated by Edwin Morgan)*
'rime' (line 9): frozen dew

Humming Bird   *Paul Groves*
'lethargy' (line 8): sleepiness
'metabolism' (line 11): the physical and chemical processes inside the body which include the changing of food into energy

with

Humming-Bird   *D. H. Lawrence*
'primeval' (line 2): from the first age of the world, before man

Blackberry-Picking   *Seamus Heaney*
'Bluebeard' (line 16): an infamous pirate

with

'In that year, 1914'   *Gary Snyder*
This poem is set in America.
'skidroad' (line 10): a road along which logs are skidded

Vergissmeinnicht   *Keith Douglas*
This poem was written during the Second World War.
'Vergissmeinnicht' (title): forget-me-not
'abased' (line 14): humbled, degraded
'swart' (line 18): black

with

Sleeper In A Valley   *Arthur Rimbaud (translated by Charles Causley)*
'cresses' (line 6): cress is a plant

'Anger lay by me all night long'   *Elizabeth Daryush*

with

A Poison Tree   *William Blake*
'wiles' (line 8): tricks

Revelation   *Liz Lochhead*
'anarchy' (line 21): absence of law

with

The Bull Moses   *Ted Hughes*
'byre' (line 3): a cowhouse

Extract from **The Destruction Of Sennacherib**   *Lord Byron*
'cohort' (line 2): a part of an army

with

Very Like A Whale   *Ogden Nash*
'Teutons' (line 3): Germans
'apoplexy' (line 9): a brainstorm
'longevity' (line 9): long life
'In heaven . . . things' (line 13): a reworking of a line from Shakespeare's
play *Hamlet* (Act 1, scene 5, line 166)
'interpolate' (line 19): to place among

Form

One way of coming to grips with the 'form' or shape of any poem is to hold it away from you until you can no longer read the words. You can still tell it is a poem because it has a distinctive shape on the page. It may be in a series of regular blocks or 'stanzas'. If so, how many are there and how many lines are there in each? Or is it a single section of verse? It clearly will not look like a block of prose from, say, a novel or a textbook. And it probably will not look like a recipe or a play or a list or a scribble.

Not only will its shape be obvious to you, but also that each poem has its own *individual* shape. You could not say the same about a list or a recipe or prose or part of a play, all of which have a standard format that rarely changes. For poetry, the actual arrangement of the words on the page is extremely important. The poet has arranged the words in this way for a reason, and the arrangement was probably (in the end, at least) conscious and deliberate.

Some poets use the visual shape of the poem on the page to good effect. You have probably seen—or written yourself—poems that adopt the shape of their subject, like this riddle of a poem by May Swenson:

> *A bloody*
> *egg yolk. A burnt hole*
> *spreading in a sheet. An en-*
> *raged rose threatening to bloom.*
> *A furnace hatchway opening, roaring.*
> *A globular bladder filling with immense*
> *juice. I start to scream. A red hydrocepha-*
> *lic* head is born, teetering on the stump of*
> *its neck. When it separates, it leaks rasp-*
> *berry from the horizon down the wide esca-*
> *lator. The cold blue boiling waves cannot*
> *scour out that band, that broadens, slid-*
> *ing toward me up the wet sand slope. The*
> *fox-hair grows, grows thicker on the*
> *upfloating head. By six o'clock,*
> *diffused to ordinary gold,*
> *it exposes each silk thread and rumple in the carpet.*

**hydrocephalic: swollen with water

The visual form here is clearly part of the intended meaning. For most poems, it is not so much the visual form in itself that is important, but the way it suggests the sound-shape of the poem. We have to remember that most poetry on the page is meant to be read and heard, and that the form of most poetry will be in sound. Try to read it aloud. Do the lines fit neatly into its shape, or are they fighting against it? Are they blurring the edges of the shape? How is the author using the form? How obvious is that form?

These questions naturally lead you on to a consideration of rhythm.

Rhythm

The English poet, Ted Hughes, has said that a poem is a 'dance of words'. Dancing, as you know, has a good deal to do with rhythm. If you've got a good sense of rhythm—of 'beat'—you'll probably be a fairly good dancer. You might find that some records are good to dance to, and that others leave you wooden at the edge of the dance floor, crying out for something more rhythmic to come on.

Edward Brathwaite, the West Indian poet, has performed some of his poems to the accompaniment of a stick beating out a rhythm—almost as if there was a drummer playing with him, establishing a 'beat'.

Octavio Paz, the Mexican poet, has said 'A poem is rhythmic language' and that the essence of any poem is its rhythm. He says, in effect, that although moment follows moment in everyday life, a poem aims to *preserve* a moment, to capture it, to save it for another time so that we can enjoy and experience it again. The poem doesn't use salt or formalin or sugar or ice to preserve that moment: it uses rhythm, repetition, *patterns* of sound, and so gives shape and identity to time.

But why are these and many other poets so concerned with rhythm? Here are some possible reasons. You may be able to think of more:

—the basic rhythm for all of us is the heartbeat: it's a (fairly!) regular beat that not only regulates our bodies, but provides a standard by which we judge other rhythms

—like the heartbeat, rhythm in dance and music and poetry is something that is immediately *felt*, that *moves* you (sometimes literally!)

—time itself (days and nights, weeks, months, seasons) has various rhythmic patterns.

It could be said that it is *rhythm* that distinguishes poetry from prose. Let's test this.

There are three very different poems in Volume 1: 'Glasgow 5 March 1971' by Edwin Morgan on page 10, 'Differences' by Günter Kunert on page 94, and 'Nursery Rhyme Of Innocence And Experience' on page 38 by Charles Causley. Hold each one at a distance from you, so that you can no longer read the words, and you'll notice that each has a distinct shape or form. They look different, and they are of different lengths. If asked, you could actually draw the shapes they make on the page.

And yet they all have at least one feature in common, and it is the feature that distinguishes them from prose: their lines do not extend to the end of the page. In fact, each poem has clear line-endings and is composed of lines of various lengths. It is as if the line itself is a deliberate unit of meaning, is meant to stand on its own and be read as something distinct: each one has a clear beginning and a clear ending to it.

In prose, of course, this is not the case. It does not matter where the line ends in a short story or a novel or a letter, because the rhythmic shape of the line is not important. If stories and novels were not printed in books with pages only a few centimetres wide, they could exist on continuous strips of paper that stretched to the moon ...

But in poems, the 'line' is essential.

Let's look at each poem in more detail.

What happens if we write out, say, Edwin Morgan's poem as if it was prose:

Quickly the magistrate has ducked to the left. The knife is just hitting the wall a few inches away. Already the police have their hands on the man in the dock whose right arm is still stretched out where the weapon left it. One feature of this picture of the Central Police Court is the striking absence of consternation.

For a start, how long those lines are depends on the size of this page. If you had a piece of paper wide enough, you could write it out in one continuous line. It wouldn't make much difference to the piece, and it might be fun to try.

But why has Edwin Morgan set it out as he has, with a break after 'magistrate'? What difference does it make in the poem to have:

> *Quickly the magistrate*
> *has ducked to the left.*

rather than:

> *Quickly the magistrate has ducked to the left.*

What difference is there to firstly, the way you read it aloud, and secondly, the meaning? And why does Morgan break up the last sentence like this:

> *One feature*
> *of this picture of the Central Police Court*
> *is the striking absence of consternation.*

Perhaps because he wanted to emphasise 'One feature' and 'striking absence of consternation'.

What about Günter Kunert's poem 'Differences'? This is what it looks like when written out as prose:

Distressed, I hear a name called out: not mine. Relieved, I hear a name called out: not mine.

Firstly, you'll notice that in the poem, the two sentences are divided by a space. Why? You'll also notice that the *pattern* of each sentence is similar. Why? What is he trying to do with these words? Thirdly, why does the first sentence have:

> *Distressed, I hear a name called out:*

and the second:

> *Relieved,*
> *I hear a name called out:*

In addressing these questions, you'll be coming to terms with the rhythm and form of the poem.

By the way, what difference would it make if Kunert's poem was set out like this:

> *Distressed,*
> *I*
> *hear*
> *a*
> *name*
> *called*
> *out:*
> *not*
> *mine.*
>
> *Relieved,*
> *I*
> *hear*
> *a*
> *name*
> *called*
> *out:*
> *not*
> *mine.*

And which version do you prefer?

Charles Causley's poem is not more rhythmical than these first two; it is simply more *regularly* rhythmical. Rhythm does not have to be a regular beat or pattern of beats. But you can see by looking at Causley's poem from a distance that there is a distinct shape to it. It is further away from prose than 'Glasgow 5 March 1971' or 'Differences', as will be clear if you write some of it out. Again, what is lost by writing it out as prose?

> *I had a silver penny and an apricot tree and I said to the sailor on the white quay 'Sailor O sailor will you bring me if I give you my money and my apricot tree a fez from Algeria an Arab drum to beat a little gilt sword and a parakeet?'*

Try this technique of writing out poems as prose and see what you lose by it. It will help you to see what is distinctive about the poem.

Talking about rhythm

Rhythm is difficult to talk about. You can *feel* it, be *moved* by it (both in your emotions and literally, on the dance floor) and enjoy it, but it is hard to find words to talk about it. Perhaps it is because it is a *physical* rather than an intellectual thing.

So here are some guidelines to help you talk about the rhythmic effects you can hear in poems.

You can distinguish between *long lines* and *short lines*, as in:

> *All day I stood there, alone on the beach,*
> *Waiting.*
> *My wet clothes clung to my skin, I felt*
> *Cold.*

Furthermore, you can distinguish between *end-stopped lines* (lines which are further reinforced at the end by a punctuation mark) like:

> *Waiting.*

or:

> *Distressed, I hear a name called out:*

and, on the other hand, *run-on lines* (lines which run on to the next one without a stop—'express' as opposed to 'local' lines) like:

> *All day, I stood there, alone on the beach*
> *Waiting.*

or:

> *One feature*
> *of this picture of the Central Police Court*
> *is the striking absence . . .*

However 'express' these run-on lines are, your *eye* can't help but register a slight pause at the end of any line, even if your voice doesn't mark it. You can talk about a *pause*, either in the middle of a line, as in:

> *The dogs. The dogs barked*
> *all night long—and drove me crazy.*

or, of course, at the end of a line:

> *This is the way the world ends*
> *Not with a bang but a whimper*

Many of these rhythmic *devices* will be used for *emphasis*, as in:

> *Quickly the magistrate*
> *has ducked to the left.*

where the new line gives emphasis to the movement. Or in the line:

> *Waiting.*

which, because it stands on its own and because you expect the line to be longer, seems to go on longer, just like waiting itself.

You will want to talk about groups of lines, as in the Kunert poem (Volume 1, p94) or the Causley (Volume 1, p38). If the lines form regular groups, as in 'Nursery Rhyme . . .', use the word *stanza*, from the Italian 'stare' meaning 'to stand'. We recommend that you avoid the word *verse* altogether here, because it can variously mean a line, a stanza, an entire poem, or poetry in general! If the lines do not form regular groups, as in the Kunert poem or in 'The Building Site' (Volume 1, p92), call those groups a *paragraph*.

Here is a list of words to help you further describe rhythm:

flowing/smooth/lilting
hypnotic
awkward/jumpy/nervous
syncopated/regular/irregular/fragmented
repetitious/repeated
heavy/ponderous/insistent
light/tripping/delicate/even
loose/tight

No doubt you will be able to think of many more!

Finally, because the word 'rhythm' is so hard to spell, here's a mnemonic (try spelling that without looking!) to help you remember it:

Remember How You Told His Mum

Imagery

We feel that poetry is a special form of communication; that it communicates moods, observations, thoughts, feelings and emotions. But what makes poetry able to do this? What tools are available to the poet so that he or she can communicate his or her feelings successfully? Perhaps the most notice-able aspect of poetry is its use of imagery. In general, poetry avoids statements of fact, such as 'Today is Monday' or 'You owe me £5' or 'Everton won again last night'; at least, it uses such statements sparingly, as starting points for a poem, for example. Instead, poetry tends to use images. An image is a picture using words instead of paint; it is a word or phrase which one can see and feel. We respond emotionally to an image but it also provides a vivid description. The actual pictures or diagrams used in a car maintenance manual are simply there to illustrate a point, to make the facts clearer, such as what a carburettor looks like and what one should turn to adjust the flow of petrol. One should not respond emotionally to such pictures; they are not there to make us feel anything. They are there to communicate facts and, if we did feel anything, it would cloud our understanding. An image in poetry should be as accurately observed as such a picture but it should also make us feel a particular emotion. Here our feelings are part of our understanding and part of the meaning.

The American poet Ezra Pound wrote many poems which are no more than simple images or juxtaposed images. One of his most famous is 'In A Station Of The Metro':

> *The apparition of these faces in the crowd;*
> *Petals on a wet, black bough.*

The first line and the title merely suggest that some faces, seen by the writer in a Paris underground station, stand out from the crowd. 'Apparition' perhaps suggests something mystical through its ghostly connotations, but there is little else beyond a simple observation. The second line does not add to the facts we have been given but the image of 'Petals on a wet, black bough', besides being an acute observation of something seen, does suggest several things:

1   The faces were suggestive of petals and thus appeared to Pound, and now to us, the readers, to be delicate and beautiful.
2   'wet, black bough' suggests that the background, out of which the faces emerged, was dark and unpleasant, possibly even a little threatening. The petals are clearly not destined to keep their beauty.
3   As petals do not grow on boughs of trees and are not usually found there, it is suggested that the particular faces noticed by Pound were out of their ordinary element.

As a whole, then, the image might be said to create a melancholic mood, joy at the delicate beauty of the faces being tempered by sadness at the transitory nature of that beauty.

Perhaps the effect of this short poem is all the stronger both for its brevity (the suggestions made by the image look very clumsy when written out as they are above) and for the unusual nature of the comparison it makes.

This leads us to the most common forms of imagery: the simile and the metaphor.

Simile & Metaphor

A simile is a figure of speech in which a similarity is expressed between two subjects directly. A simile is introduced by either 'like'; for example, 'She runs like a panther', or by 'as'; for example, 'She is as slow as a snail'.

A metaphor is a figure of speech in which a similarity is expressed between two subjects indirectly. 'He laughed like a donkey' is a simile; but 'He brayed with laughter' is a metaphor. One realises this as soon as one recognises that 'to bray' means to make a noise like a donkey. Edward Thomas's phrase 'The great diamonds of rain' in 'It Rains' (p11) is a metaphor: the poet sees a similarity between raindrops and diamonds which could have been expressed as a simile. How?

e e cummings's poem 'she being Brand' (p32) is an extended metaphor; the comparison between a woman and a car is developed throughout the poem. This is also the case with Theodore Roethke's 'The Geranium' (p28) where the comparison between the geranium and a woman is developed all through the poem.

A well-chosen simile or metaphor expresses a great deal in a few words. 'She runs like a panther' for example, suggests that not only is 'she' a fast runner but that 'she' is also a sleek, beautiful and powerful runner (all qualities of a panther), possessing a feline grace. One of the tasks of the reader of poetry is to trace all the suggestions in a simile or metaphor which are relevant. For instance, in the above simile, it would clearly not be relevant to suggest that 'she' has a furry coat or dangerous claws, although a panther has both these things. The reason for this is simple: in that simile the woman ('she') and the panther are being compared in terms of running; a panther's coat and claws are clearly not relevant to what we notice about how it looks when it is running.

When the Duke Orsino, in Shakespeare's play *Twelfth Night*, says that his love for Olivia is 'as hungry as the sea' he is not suggesting that his love is blue or green or whatever colour one thinks that the sea is. He is, however, suggesting that his love has the vastness of the sea as well as its ability to swallow up anything and its threatening, destructive power.

When Henry Reed in 'Naming Of Parts' (p30) writes that 'Japonica glistens like coral' he is not suggesting that the flower Japonica has sharp edges, like coral; he is, however, suggesting that the Japonica has an intense, shining and exotic beauty, like coral. We often use similes and metaphors in our own speech and writing, usually without thinking. Popular similes and metaphors become clichés: phrases which we do not have to stop and think about and which, because they have been overused, have lost any real meaning they may once have had. 'As sick as a parrot' is one such simile; 'smooth as silk', 'like greased lightning' and 'as cold as ice' are three others. We have heard them so often that they no longer have the power to mean any more than 'unhappy', 'smooth', 'fast' and 'cold' respectively. A careful writer, and one should recognise that poets are, or ought to be, very careful writers, will try to use similes and metaphors which are fresh and full of suggestions which are vital to the poet's meaning, as we shall see.

Let us examine a few lines of Shakespeare, from his play *Antony and Cleopatra*. Here Antony is convinced that he has lost the battle against Octavius Caesar, the Roman emperor; he has thus also lost Cleopatra and his own empire and, during a soliloquy, he says the following lines:

> The hearts
> That spaniel'd me at heels, to whom I gave
> Their wishes, do discandy, melt their sweets
> On blossoming Caesar: and this pine is barked
> That overtopped them all.

One might simply paraphrase this speech as follows: 'All my friends have deserted me for Caesar. I am no longer a powerful figure'. In a sense, that is all that Antony means. Yet, if we examine the imagery he employs, especially the metaphors, we will see that he says much more than the above paraphrase. 'The hearts' of Antony's followers suggests their central, most vital part. The heart is often regarded as the source of true feeling and affection (the phrase 'with all my heart' suggests absolute conviction of feeling) and thus this opening image creates the idea that Antony's followers have been genuinely faithful to him before his defeat and that now he has lost them completely.

Not only does 'Spaniel'd' suggest the dog-like devotion of Antony's followers but the devotion of a particular dog, a spaniel; a dog renowned for its gentle, affectionate nature. 'At heels' develops the image of the obedient, subservient, faithful nature of his followers and the phrase as a whole suggests that there was a mutual sense of fulfilment in the relationship. Thus, through three metaphors ('hearts', 'spaniel'd' and 'at heels'), we are made to feel how Antony felt about his followers and their departure. 'Discandy' suggests a loss of sweetness, as if Antony's previous sweet, and thus happy, position is changing (and note how it suggests how sweet that relationship between Antony and his men was). This is developed by 'melt their sweets' as if Antony is now left alone, bereft of sweetness, which is now gently (suggested by 'melt') covering Caesar. Caesar is 'blossoming', which suggests that he is at the most fruitful time of his life, as well as suggesting that there is now a natural and attractive beauty about him. In contrast, Antony feels that he himself is a 'pine' that is 'barked': stripped of bark, as he is stripped of his followers, and thus on the way to dying. A powerful feeling of Antony's loneliness is created. Yet 'this pine' once 'overtopped them all' and we have a poignant image of Antony as he was: the dominant figure in the political landscape, towering over all around him. The contrasts, then, between Antony's perception of himself before and now, between the 'blossoming' growing Caesar and the 'barked' dying Antony, are incredibly strong and effective. We too feel his sense of loss and worthlessness.

His followers have been seen as hearts, spaniels, sweet things, bark and other trees. Each of these images (and metaphors) suggests feelings and ideas about Antony's relationship with them, with himself, and with Caesar; and these images are neither clichéd nor too disconnected from each other. We can see that the imagery does not just add to the meaning: the imagery *is* the meaning. The paraphrase from which we started is utterly inadequate and barely begins to say what Antony has said; it does not begin to suggest what Antony feels about his followers, Casear, or himself. Unless we examine the imagery and see what it suggests, we can have no idea of the depth and complexity of the emotion that Antony is expressing. For, as has been said earlier, what matters in poetry is not the facts that are revealed but the emotions.

Approaching the Unseen Poem

Many English Literature examinations feature a poem that you will not have seen before. Some guidelines may be provided to help you write about the poem but these may not be enough in themselves. We hope that the following guidelines may be of more help to you. We suggest that you consider them more or less in the order they are presented.

1 When you first see the poem, don't panic. Poems often look difficult at first but, after careful reading and some thought, they become much clearer. However, even after careful study there may still be lines that you feel you do not fully 'understand'. This is not something you should worry about. See point *6*.

2 Read the poem carefully but not too slowly, as if you were reading it aloud in public. Try to get a feel of it as a whole; don't worry about lines or phrases that you don't immediately grasp and don't let your mind linger on them. Concentrate on the line that you're reading rather than on the lines you've just read.

3 Consider the title: titles are often very important and can provide a vital insight into what the poem is about.

4 Read the poem again, slowly and carefully, bearing the title in mind. Remember that you cannot read a poem as if it were a novel or short story: much more concentration and attention to detail are needed.

5 Decide what the situation of the poem is: who is speaking and to whom? Under what circumstances? Is the poem thoughtful or dramatic?

6 Try to decide what the theme or idea of the poem is; what the poem, in other words, is about. Remember the importance of the title. If you are asked to comment on the 'theme or idea of the poem', you have to say what you think it is but you might also say which parts of the poem, including the title, most clearly suggest the theme. If there are words or phrases that are still puzzling you, think about what they suggest that might be relevant to the theme.

7 What is the tone of the poem? If you were reading it aloud, what tone of voice would you use? Would you change your tone at any point?

8 Once you have dealt with these questions, you can consider and prepare to comment on:

—use of simile and metaphor—what do they suggest that is relevant to the theme? If the question asks you to comment on 'interesting and effective uses of language' or on 'words and phrases that you find interesting', you might concentrate on similes and metaphors and show what they suggest about their subject.

—use of rhythm, rhyme and the way the words are laid out on the page— what words and phrases are given emphasis by the rhythm or the rhyme (or the lack of a rhyme where we expect one) or by the way the words are laid out on the page? Why are those particular words/phrases given emphasis?

—use of alliteration and assonance—again, what words and phrases are given emphasis by these techniques? Why are these particular words and phrases emphasised?

9 You should now be in a position to say whether or not you like the poem and be able to give some reasons for your feelings.

What follows is an example of an examination essay on an unseen poem. You may want to read it and gain an idea both of how to organise and express your ideas in essay form. You may, however, prefer to ignore what follows and find your own way of writing and organising an essay: we should emphasise that there are many perfectly correct ways of writing any essay. How we have done it is only a suggestion.

Essay on 'Mama And Daughter' by Langston Hughes

This poem consists of a conversation between a mother and her daughter. The daughter is preparing to go and meet her 'sugar-sweet' and the mother is helping her to get ready. The poem is dramatic: the conversation is written down in direct speech and it could easily be performed by two speakers. Such a performance would be a very effective way of reading the poem. Remarks like, 'I'll brush behind' and 'Your father, yes, he was the one!' almost demand to be read aloud; and the layout of the poem makes it impossible not to realise that there are two speakers. The title makes it clear who they are.

The daughter is going out with a young man and her strong feelings for him are suggested by her referring to him as her 'sugar-sweet'. This is a rather clichéd expression and makes us feel that the daughter is not very old. Her mention of her boy-friend causes her mother, who has been naturally inquisitive but eager to help, to think back to her own past. She begins as if she is telling a story: 'Once upon a time' but she remembers her husband and passion enters her voice: 'Yes, he was the one!' Although she admits 'it was a long time ago' her anger at being deserted clearly has not faded as she refers to him passionately as a 'wild son-of-a-gun' and hopes that he 'Rots in hell today!' The exclamation marks emphasise her anger.

It comes as a shock that the father has deserted his family—we do not realise it until line 14—but the daughter is calm about what her mother

148

has said and simply points out that he 'couldn't still be young'. Perhaps the mother does not like being corrected or perhaps she is very unhappy about her memories but she reacts angrily and the gentle tone of line 6 is replaced by the much more violent 'Turn around!/So I can brush your back, I say!' We can see how she does not want to accept what has happened by the emphasis on 'was' in lines 18 and 19.

There is no use of simile or metaphor apart from the phrase 'sugar-sweet' in the poem which helps to confirm the idea of two people talking: people do not often use similes and metaphors in their speech. The regular rhythms and rhymes in the poem make it flow quickly which emphasises the dramatic effect.

I like the poem very much as it gives me a strong impression of characters and their family situation in so few words. I particularly like the way the mother begins her story calmly, breaks off to say 'Let me brush the hem', showing she is still thinking of her daughter, but then becomes so involved in her story that she loses her temper.

Ideas for Coursework Folders

You will find here not only ideas for your Literature coursework folder, but also for your folder or for classwork in English Language. You should, of course, check with your teacher what the particular requirements of your syllabus are before you start. There may be a word limit or a specific style in which you are asked to write. These ideas will be suitable for most syllabuses.

1   Selection of 6–10 poems by theme
Once you have selected poems based on a common theme (and the index on p152 will help you), you should concentrate your notes on the differences between the poems as well as on their similarities. You might mention mood, tone, intensity of feeling, degree of detail, form, and what you think the writer's intention is. You might be able to group them in various ways, and may wish to say which of the poems you have chosen (you don't have to limit yourself to the poems in this anthology) you think is the most successful. This could, if you wanted it to, become a longer piece of writing for your folder, and might link with the actual making of your own anthology.

2 Selection of poems by one poet

In this anthology there is a section devoted to three poets: John Betjeman, Sylvia Plath and Langston Hughes. On the other hand, if there is another particular poet in this volume or elsewhere that you enjoy you might like to find more of his or her poems and write about them. Ask your teacher and/or librarian for help.

3 Selection of poems by region or culture

There are poems in this anthology by writers from Scotland, Ireland, England, Australia, the West Indies, the USA, Africa, India, Malaysia, Poland, France, Russia, Japan, Finland, Chile, Mexico, East Germany and China. You may wish to find more poems from one of these countries and to see if you can identify any common characteristics between them. Again, you could make your own anthology before your start this kind of writing.

4 Selection of poems by form

Another way to group poems is by their form (that is to say, by the way the words are arranged on the page; see *Glossary*).

5 Writing about one poem

The 'key' poems in this anthology are provided with full notes to help you gain a richer response to them. You may wish to take one of them and write about it in one of various ways: (a) you could write a personal account of how you have come to a fuller understanding of the poem after several readings (b) you could write a more formal analysis of the poem or (c) you could give reasons as to why you prefer it to other poems in the anthology.

Of course, you could choose *any* poem to write about, as long as there is enough to write about it. To ensure you have enough to write, you should choose a poem of some substance.

6 Comparing two or three poems

Taking two or three poems to compare is probably easier than writing about just one poem, because you will be able to note the similarities and differences between the poems. You could take poems in any of the four categories mentioned in 1–4 above, or select two or three poems that have less in common. Section 5, Poems for Comparison gives you a start.

7 Comparing poetry with prose

'Prose' is ordinary spoken and written language in a direct, straightforward arrangement, as opposed to poetry where there is a conscious rhythmic arrangement of words to convey a feeling or idea. Stories, novels, letters and these notes are written in prose. Prose only breaks into lines because the edge of the page won't allow it to go any further.

There are at least two possible ways in which you can compare poetry with prose: (a) you could take one of the poems in the anthology and re-write it as if it were prose, then make notes as to what is lost by this 'translation' or (b) you could find a passage of prose—or write one yourself for that matter!—on the same theme as one of the poems, and then compare the two pieces of writing.

If you want a piece of prose for your English folder, you could write an 'answer' to one of the poems here, or write on a similar theme. It may be possible for you to include some poetry in your English folder too, but you should check with your teacher before you attempt this.

8 Presenting a selection of poems

Which poems in this anthology would you select if you had to introduce poetry to a new reader? You would want to provide a wide range of types, and could write an interlinking text to help introduce them. This piece of work need not confine itself to your coursework folder, but could form the basis of a live or recorded talk.

9 Recorded discussion

Take any of the approaches suggested above, and rather than aim toward a written account, use the approach as the basis for a taped discussion with a small group of fellow-students. You may then wish to write down the discussion, and edit it for inclusion in your folder. This will be an interesting exercise in itself, and will teach you a great deal about how people discuss and something of the relationship between speech and writing.

10 Reading the poems aloud

You may like to try reading one of the poems in at least two ways, shedding a different light on the poem with each reading. Having recorded the readings, you could write a piece comparing their qualities and the aspects of the poem they emphasise.

Suggested Cross-referencing by Theme

Glossary

Alliteration: the repetition of the same initial sound in words close together; 'pennies and pounds' or 'the golden goose' are both examples of alliteration. Alliteration is often used in advertisements for much the same purpose that it is used in poetry.

Assonance: similar, but not identical, vowel sounds. Identical vowel and final consonant sounds create *rhyme*; for example, 'good' and 'should' rhyme; 'shook' and 'should' do not rhyme but the similar vowel sound between them is an example of assonance. Assonance only occurs within the line.

Ballad: ballads would originally have been sung or recited. They were once a very popular form of entertainment and one of the characteristics of ballads is that they tell stories. Ballads nearly always have a very regular rhythm and rhyme scheme.

Dramatic monologue: a poem written as though it is being spoken by one person, usually to another who does not speak. The speaker, while talking of other things, reveals a great deal about his or her character.

Form: the shape and structure of a poem; the way the words are arranged on the page. In many poems there is a regular form; the poet may have used four line stanzas consisting of ten syllable lines, for instance. Rhyme may well play a part in determining the form of a poem: a poem may be written in rhyming couplets, for instance (lines that rhyme in pairs). A poem may well not have a regular form; in other words, the form is irregular. See *Form* on p138.

Image: usually a picture in words; a phrase which is meant to make one visualise or experience what is being described.

Imagery: the use of figurative language, usually simile, metaphor or personification. See *Imagery* on p143 and Thom Gunn's introduction on p27.

Metaphor: a comparison *not* introduced by 'like' or 'as'; for example, 'he was a stubborn mule in the argument' is a metaphor whereas 'he argued like a stubborn mule' is a simile. Note that neither the simile nor the metaphor suggest that 'he' had any mulish qualities (such as four legs) apart from a mule's stubbornness and, possibly, stupidity. See *Simile & Metaphor* on p144.

Narrative: a story; the telling of a story, which usually involves characters engaged in doing something.

Parody: a parody imitates the form, style, thought or words of another, usually serious, work. It is intended to make fun of the original on which it is based.

Persona: the narrator or speaker of a poem; that part of one's character that one chooses to present to the rest of the world. You would assume a different persona when speaking to your head teacher from the one you might assume when speaking to a child younger than you.

154

Personification: giving human characteristics, such as speech or personality, to animals, objects or ideas.

Rhyme: similarity of sound based on vowels preceded by different consonants, as with 'dog' and 'log'. Rhyme usually occurs at line-endings but can also occur at the beginning or in the middle of lines. Also note *pararhyme* in which the vowel sounds are different but the consonant sounds before and after the vowels are the same, e.g. 'pleading' and 'plodding'.

Rhythm: all words, when spoken, have a rhythm; that is, a number of stressed syllables and a number of unstressed syllables, for one cannot avoid stressing some of the syllables. The stressed syllables create a rhythm. In poetry, as in music, the rhythm is often regular in which case one can call it 'metre'. See *Rhythm* on p139.

Setting: the background against which the main action of a poem takes place. The setting may be (a) geographical—where the poem is set (b) the time—of day, of year or even the year itself—the poem is set (c) the social world from which the poem's speaker or characters come or (d) any combination of these elements.

Simile: a comparison introduced by 'like' or 'as', for example 'She ran like the wind' or 'The rain was as cold as ice'. See *Simile & Metaphor* on p144.

Situation: the situation of a poem refers to the speakers and/or characters in the poem, the relationship, if any, between them (who is speaking to whom, for example) and the position that they are in. The situation in '"He Shot Arrows But Not At Birds Perching"', for example, is that the speaker of the poem and a Governor are at the former's farm and are spending time with one another. One might go on to speculate, on the evidence of the poem, that the two are friends.

Stanza: a division, usually but not always regular, of a poem. Sometimes, when the stanzas are not regular, they are referred to as *paragraphs*. A stanza is sometimes referred to as a *verse*.

Subject: what the poem is about on the surface, as opposed to what it is really about, which is called *theme*. For example, the subject of 'The Mosquito Knows' is a mosquito; but for the theme of that poem, see below.

Syllable: a syllable is one single sound. 'Dog' has one syllable; 'rabbit' has two ('rab' and 'bit'); porcupine has three ('por', 'cu' and 'pine').

Theme: the main idea expressed by a poem or the main idea with which the poem is concerned. For instance, one of the themes of D. H. Lawrence's 'The Mosquito Knows' has to do with people's greed for money.

Tone: it is easiest to determine tone by reading the poem aloud. Just as any phrase—'How are you?' for example—can be spoken in several very different tones of voice (and thus imply several very different emotions), so one must read a poem carefully to determine its tone. Remember that the tone might change during the course of the poem.

Index of Poets

Acknowledgements

The editors and publishers wish to thank the following for permission to reproduce poems:

Jaakko Ahokas for 'Winter Is Here' by Katri Vala from *The Penguin Book of Women Poets*; Allison & Busby for 'English Scene' by Adrian Mitchell from *For Beauty Douglas*; Angus & Robertson for 'Because' by James McAuley from *Collected Poems* © James McAuley 1971; Anvil Press Poetry Ltd for 'The Potato Patch' by E. A. Markham; Bogle L'Ouverture Publications Ltd for 'Desire' and 'Military Two-Step' by Cecil Rajendra from *Hour of Assassins*; Cape Publishers for 'Naming Of Parts' by Henry Reed from *A Map of Verona*; Carcanet Press Limited for 'The Moons of Jupiter: Europa' by Edwin Morgan from *Poems of Thirty Years*, '"Anger lay by me all night long"' by Elizabeth Daryush, 'Red Wheelbarrow' by William Carlos Williams from *Collected Earlier Poems*, 'Selling Watermelons' by Andrei Voznesensky and 'Winter Night' by Boris Pasternak from *Doctor Zhivago*, translations by Edwin Morgan from *Rites of Passage*; 'One Flesh' and 'Absence' by Elizabeth Jennings from *Selected Poems*; Nicholas Christopher for 'Cardiac Arrest' from the '*The New Yorker*'; Chatto & Windus Ltd for 'Monotony' and 'Waiting For The Barbarians' by C. P. Cavafy from *C. P. Cavafy Collected Poems* trans. by Edmund Keeley and Philip Sherrard, also by permission of Mrs Songopoulo, 'Dulce Et Decorum Est' by Wilfred Owen from *The Collected Poems of Wilfred Owen* edited by C. D. Lewis, also by permission of the author's literary estate; J.M. Dent & Sons Ltd for 'Holidays In Childhood' by Clifford Dyment from *The Axe in the Wood*; Dell Publishing Co Inc © 1972 for 'I'm Explaining A Few Things' by Pablo Neruda from *Selected Poems* translated by Alastair Reid, edited by Nathaniel Tarn © 1970 by Anthony Kerrigan, W. S. Merwin, Alastair Reid and Nathaniel Tarn, reprinted by permission of Delacorte Press/Seymour Lawrence; Marie J. Douglas for 'Vergissmeinnicht' by Keith Douglas from *The Complete Poems of Keith Douglas* edited by Desmond Graham (1978) by permission of Oxford University Press; Faber & Faber Ltd for 'The Geranium' by Theodore Roethke from *The Collected Poems of Theodore Roethke*, 'Blackberry Picking' from *Death of a Naturalist* by Seamus Heaney, 'Cleator Moor' from *Five Rivers* by Norman Nicholson, '"And the days are not full enough"' from *Lustra* by Ezra Pound, from *Collected Shorter Poems*, 'Work And Play' and 'The River In March' from *Seasons Songs* by Ted Hughes, 'The Bull Moses' and 'Hawk Roosting' from *Lupercal* by Ted Hughes, 'Preludes' by T. S. Eliot from *Collected Poems 1909-1962*, 'To The Public' by Louis MacNeice from *The Collected Poems of Louis MacNeice*, 'Epitaph On A Tyrant' and 'The Unknown Citizen' from *Collected Poems* by W. H. Auden, 'A Study Of Reading Habits' by Philip Larkin from *The Whitsun Weddings*; Sarah Goossens for 'Politics'; Paul Groves for 'Humming Bird' from *Poetry Introductions 3* (Faber & Faber); David Higham Associates Ltd for 'Ballad Of The Landlord' and 'Delinquent' by Langston Hughes from *Selected Poems of Langston Hughes (Alfred A. Knopf, Inc)*, '*I Saw A Jolly Hunter*' by Charles Causley from *Collected Poems*

157

(Macmillan), 'One Flesh' and 'Absence' by Elizabeth Jennings from *Selected Poems* (Carcanet Press); Richard Hill for 'Tombstone Library'; The Hogarth Press for 'Brooklyn Cop' from *Rings On A Tree* by Norman MacCaig; Olwyn Hughes for 'Southern Sunrise', 'Fiesta Melons', 'Mushrooms', 'You're', 'Morning Song', 'Blackberrying', 'Mirror' by Sylvia Plath (Faber & Faber Collections) © Ted Hughes; Indiana University Press for 'The Street' by Octavio Paz from *Early Poems 1935–1955*; Evan Jones for 'Song Of The Banana Man' from *West Indian Poetry* (ILEA); Alfred A. Knopf Inc for 'Puzzled', 'Mama And Daughter', 'S-sss-ss-sh', 'Hard Daddy', 'Little Old Letter', 'Ruby Brown' by Langston Hughes from *Selected Poems of Langston Hughes*, © Langston Hughes 1959; Little Brown & Co Inc for 'Adventures Of Isabel' and 'Very Like A Whale' by Ogden Nash; Liveright Pub. Corporation Inc for 'she being Brand' by e e cummings from *Poems 1923–1954*; James MacGibbon for 'Not Waving But Drowning' by Stevie Smith from *The Collected Poems of Stevie Smith* (Penguin Modern Classics); Macmillan Publishers, USA, for 'Four Glimpses Of Night' by Frank Marshall Davis from *Beowulf to Beatles* edited by Pichaske (The Free Press); Una Marson for 'Darlingford' from *West Indian Poetry* (ILEA); Mbari Publications for 'Night Rain' by John Pepper Clark; Methuen London for 'Everything New Is Better Than Everything Old' by Bertolt Brecht trans. by Christopher Middleton from *Poems 1913–1956*; North Point Press for '"He Shot Arrows, But Not At Birds Perching"' from *Axe Handles* © by Gary Snyder 1983; John Murray Publishers for 'Hunter Trials', 'Pot Pourri From A Surrey Garden', 'Indoor Games Near Newbury', 'Executive', 'Death In Leamington', 'Senex' by John Betjeman; Oxford University Press and Watson, Little Ltd as licensing agents for 'Buy One Now' from *Sad Ires* (*Collected Poems*) by D. J. Enright, 'What The Chairman Told Tom' from *Basil Bunting, Collected Poems* © Basil Bunting, 'A Consumer's Report' from *Peter Porter, Collected Poems* © Peter Porter; Polygon Books for 'Revelation' by Liz Lochead; Penguin Books Ltd for 'Late Summer' by Kinoshita Yuji from *The Penguin Book of Japanese Verse*, translation and introduction by Geoffrey Bownas and Anthony Thwaite, 1964, 'Listen To Me' by Kishwar Naheed from *The Penguin Book Of Modern Urdu Poetry* selected and translated by Mahmood Jamal, 1986, 'Opposition' by Kaneko Mitsuharu from *The Penguin Book of Japanese Verse*, translation and introduction by Geoffrey Bownas and Anthony Thwaite (Penguin Books, 1964), 'Palm-Tree' by Rabindranath Tagore from *Selected Poems of Rabindranath Tagore* translated by William Radice (Penguin Modern Classics, 1985); Secker & Warburg Ltd for 'Common Sense' by Alan Brownjohn from *Sandgrains on a Tray*, 'Brief Thoughts On Exactness' by Miroslav Holub from *Notes of a Clay Pigeon*, 'Picture Of A Girl' by James Lasdun from *A Jump Start*; Gary Snyder for 'In that year, 1914 . . .' from *A Range of Poems*; Myfanwy Thomas for 'Digging' and 'It Rains' by Edward Thomas from *Collected Poems* (Faber & Faber); Nicholas Christopher for 'Cardiac Arrest' from *A Short History of the Island of Butterflies*; Karol Wojtyla for '"That world will come like a thief"'

Whilst every effort has been made to contact the copyright holders, this has not proved to be possible in every case.